LABOUR PAINS

LABOUR PAINS

How the party I love lost its soul

Peter Kilfoyle

First published in Great Britain in 2010 by
Biteback Publishing Ltd
Heal House
375 Kennington Lane
London
SE11 5QY

ISBN 978-1-84954-035-3

1 3 5 7 9 10 8 6 4 2

A CIP catalogue record for this book is available from the British Library.

Set in Minion by SoapBox, www.soapboxcommunications.co.uk

Printed and bound in Great Britain by TJ International Ltd

one

O happy day! July 4 1991, Independence Day, and the day on which I was elected to Parliament following a difficult by-election. Glorious sunshine greeted my win and I was exuberant, as much with relief that the by-election campaign was over, as with any sense of triumph.

The media coverage had been intense and, for a few short weeks, it seemed as if the political universe revolved around the streets of Liverpool Walton. It had certainly been a tremendous experience, and is one which notoriously gives candidates (and sometimes their wives) a false sense of their importance in the political scheme of things.

Of course, I was no different. It was planned that I would arrive with my wife and family to be sworn in on the Tuesday following my election. In those days, Prime Minister's Questions were held on Tuesdays and Thursdays. My planned arrival on the Tuesday was intended to give a message to the Tories that their days in office were numbered. This was a tad presumptuous as they were eventually to go on to a surprise victory at the following general election.

As we arrived at the Commons, we were met by the then leader of the opposition, Neil Kinnock. Naturally, he wanted to milk the occasion for all the publicity he could get. I understood and expected that. What I had not anticipated was the number of staff who greeted me by name as I passed through the building. It reinforced my misconception that my election mattered in itself, and that I might make a mark in the House. By the end of the next day, that illusion was to be shattered.

I was escorted into the chamber to take the oath by two friends, Mo Mowlam and George Howarth. John Major eyed me up and down as I took the oath, standing directly in front of him. Once the formalities were done, I took a seat in the chamber for a while and then left. A pleasant afternoon followed with my family on the terrace, enjoying tea and scones, before they departed for home in Liverpool and I began my parliamentary career.

That was it. I was on my own from there on in. No formal induction, no advice, other than that which I gleaned by chance from colleagues. No one told me about offices or phones or mail. I was simply left to get on with things as best I could. It was as if I had been dropped in a completely unknown country without money, a map or a phrase book. Even the staff who had welcomed me on the first day appeared to be intent on now putting me in my place, telling me what it was I ought to do at each turn.

Yet, being a quick learner, I busied myself organising mail and finding my way around the Palace of Westminster. Some colleagues were helpful in responding to my questions; most were sublimely indifferent to both my presence and my very existence as an honourable member. It was truly sink or swim. The whips were of no use whatsoever – they would not allocate me an office or a telephone – so I learnt to rely on my own wits for everything. After all, Labour would be in government at the next election – or so I and most of the Labour Party believed – and things would improve then, both inside and outside Parliament. How wrong I was to be!

* * *

John Major was the last person the Labour Party expected to succeed the loathed Mrs Thatcher. I suspect most Tories discounted his chances as well, yet he became Prime Minister in her place. On our side, we were convinced that he would fall at the next general election. Our own 'dream ticket' of Neil Kinnock and Roy Hattersley would lead Labour to victory after thirteen years of Tory hegemony.

They were a very odd couple indeed, both in personality and in politics. Together it was hoped that they would bind the two political wings of the Labour Party together in an electorally advantageous way. Roy Hattersley represented the old right of Labour and was widely appreciated for not having defected to the SDP with some of his former political and ideological soul mates. Neil Kinnock had put behind him his days as a left-wing firebrand. He was now focused on one objective: making the Labour Party electable. This pairing could not have been more different from the Blair–Brown diarchy that was eventually to succeed them.

Neil had built up a formidable office staff to help him in his crusade to turn Labour around. It included Charles Clarke, who was to eventually reach the Cabinet, along with two others who soared to similar heights: Patricia Hewitt, who became a secretary of state, and Jan Royall, who became leader of the House of Lords. Sue Nye was eventually to transfer her loyalty to Gordon Brown and remains there to this day, hugely influential, as his 'gatekeeper'. If you want to get to Gordon, you need Sue on side.

Roy had a smaller operation. His loyal adviser was David Hill, later to take Alastair Campbell's place as the Prime Minister's spokesman. David's wife, Hilary Coffman, was a press officer to Neil Kinnock. It was all very comfortable as the party aimed to take over the reins of government.

We backbenchers saw our role as harrying the government at every turn. It was not so difficult. Firstly, there were some intensely dislikeable Tories on the government benches whom I instinctively found quite repulsive. There were others who struck me as simply crackers. Naturally, we had our own eccentrics, but that was the point: they may have been nutters, but they were *our* nutters. Besides, the tremendous antagonism towards Mrs Thatcher was transferred to all Tories, so great was Labour dislike of her and of all she stood for.

These were days when the principal weapon of Her Majesty's Loyal Opposition was time. Essentially, we tried to keep the government up as long into the night as possible. The theory was that we could exhaust ministers into making catastrophic mistakes at their Whitehall desks by keeping them up all hours. This assumed that Labour members were up for this war of attrition. Many were: as long as the House was sitting, the bars were open, and the foot solders in the war were men (mainly men) from distant parts of the United Kingdom with nothing else to do with their time. There were others who became noticeable by their absence from these endeavours, either because they needed their beauty sleep, or they had other interests – both social and business – outside the guerrilla tactics of opposition in the House. I became more acutely aware of these particular 'usual suspects' later when I became a whip.

It remained for me a fascinating place, full of characters. Many of these I had met, but did not pretend to know. I recall the surprise in Denis Healey's voice as he relayed his discovery of a toilet near his office which he had never known existed. I was also honoured to sit on the same benches as Michael Foot, who had first joined the Labour Party after having seen the poverty of Liverpool. Mrs Thatcher, of course, was an immense presence on the Tory back benches, alongside many of those whom she had promoted and then demoted. I found the chamber a fantastically educative piece of theatre. I did not always feel the same about the rest of Parliament.

Within days of being sworn in, I attended the Press Bar at the invitation of some journalists who had covered my by-election. One journalist set out to be provocative with nasty comments about a member of my family. My instinct was to thump him. George Howarth advised me to ignore him and I did. I have to assume that the hack in question was deliberately trying to set me up to do just what I had considered – that would have been a story. I resolved thereafter always to be wary of lobby journalists.

Many of my colleagues were equally difficult to deal with, but for different reasons. Take, for example, the Scottish member Tommy Graham. His accent was incredibly thick, and I speak as the proud owner of a Scouse accent. One Friday morning, we were debating Sir Ivan Lawrence's private member's bill on a possible national lottery. I spoke early on in the debate – I had a big pools interest in my constituency. Tommy arrived late, but eventually was called to speak. He was amazing. I could barely understand a word he spoke, other than the odd reference to 'a loaf of bread', 'a pint of milk'. I noticed that the Hansard writers in the gallery sat back and listened without taking any notes. When he finished, Tommy asked me: 'Well, what did y'think?'

I answered truthfully if diplomatically: 'In truth, Tommy, I have never heard a speech like it.'

He seemed happy enough, and then took a typed speech out of his inside pocket and sent it up to the Hansard writers. Tommy had not used a word of it, apparently, but he had an agreement with Hansard that he would always send his typed speeches to them, as they too could not understand a word he said. He employed a man to write speeches for him which he never gave, but they always looked articulate and erudite in Hansard!

This was all part of my apprenticeship in a House which still had the power to beguile me. I still believed that it was a collection of people dedicated first and foremost to improving the lives of their constituents, regardless of party label. For many – indeed, most – that was the case. However, a large minority of my fellow MPs were propelled by their egos in a quest for personal gain. Nothing revealed this better to me than the first election of Labour's parliamentary committee – better known as the shadow Cabinet.

It struck me that there were two broad groups standing for these positions. The first group consisted of the alleged 'big hitters' – people who assumed that they had an automatic right to be in a senior position. I included in this group people like John Smith, Robin Cook and Jack Cunningham. There were others who were 'wannabes' – often able and diligent, but lacking that extra something which marked out the political stars. This group included the likes of David Clark, Tom Clarke and Barry Jones.

Most candidates had a little team of acolytes working for them, dropping a word in here and there to possibly supportive voters in the election, held by the Parliamentary Labour Party. I saw this as a demeaning role, hawking defective goods from member to member. Each candidate had a different approach. Barry Jones operated throughout the year, sending members birthday cards and notes congratulating them on some obscure speech. He hoped that this investment would pay off in the annual elections. David Clark's approach was quite clever. He asked members to give him a spare vote 'so I will not be humiliated'. It invariably worked in getting him re-elected to the shadow Cabinet.

What struck me about the process was that it had nothing to do with talent, or aptitude for the job. It was just a political beauty contest, without the beauty. There was another key factor which was disturbing – the role of the Whips' Office, and one whip in particular: Ray Powell, the member for Ogmore.

This little Welshman managed to wield the votes of about twenty members. Quite simply, it was political corruption. Members – including the Militant members – were given time off by Powell for their various activities (he was the pairing whip) in return for their votes. This gave him enormous influence within the PLP and ensured that some wholly unsuitable individuals made it into the shadow Cabinet.

I had felt this man's anger soon after being elected. I went to see him about a desk or an office – he was responsible also for accommodation. He gave me short shrift, annoyed that, prior to coming to Parliament, I had complained to Neil Kinnock about the ease with which Militant MP Terry Fields was covered by the whips office for his Militant activities. The *Sunday Times* had run a story on this issue, for which Fields threatened me with court action. There was no way that Powell was going to help me. There was even less chance when I supported Ron Davies, who was standing against him for his whip's job. Interestingly, I asked the then backbenchers whether they would be voting for change. Their answers varied, but few gave a direct response. They presumably had too much to lose by being honest.

No office was a problem. My neighbouring MP – Bob Parry – had been in Parliament for twenty-seven years without an office or a phone. Referred to as the 'member for Pyongyang', for he was very close to the leader of North Korea, Kim Il Sung, he was not a role model that I aspired to emulate. Help was at hand, however, in the unlikely shape of Ted Leadbitter, member for Hartlepool, who was due to retire at the following election. He offered me his half-share of a room with Roger Stott, member for Wigan. I needed it more than he did, Ted kindly stated.

Sharing with Roger was itself an experience. Very much liked by his north-west colleagues, he remained a naive soul to his dying day. His gullibility was exploited in a good-natured way by his colleagues on an almost daily basis. Laurence Cunliffe, the member for Leigh, had the complete measure of Roger and set him up for prank after prank. Yet there was never any malice. The spirit generally in the PLP was a happy one, as we all pulled together towards the next general election.

Taking the north-west as an example, the PLP had not yet suffered the demographic shift that was to change the very nature of the Labour Party and give us the corruption that was New Labour. There were many traditional working-class members: Roger and Laurence I have mentioned, but also Stan Orme, Ken Eastham, Bob Litherland, Eddie Loyden, Joe Benton, John Evans and many others. It was a party in which people like myself could feel comfortable.

We even instituted an annual 'works outing' under the aegis of 'The Strangers' Bar Choir'. This took the form of a Christmas dinner and continues to this day, but without, in my view, the brio of the early years.

The name 'Choir' came from the habit of having a sing-along in the Strangers' Bar in the late, late hours as we awaited votes. In those days, of course, we could be kept in the House for voting throughout the night. No liberal use of guillotine motions then. Choirmaster was Black Country MP Dennis Turner. A very popular man – now Lord Bilston – Dennis had the endearing habit of compering the entertainment in his local Springvale Social Club each Saturday night, when he also acted as bingo caller. A man without any pretensions, unlike many in the House.

Having worked closely with Neil Kinnock's office during the Militant years, I kept up my contacts with them, fully expecting that they would be the core team in 10 Downing Street after the next general election, due in May 1992. Needless to say, they were all working flat out to secure a Labour government. There were, of course, hiccups on the way. The presentational axis of Peter Mandelson and Philip Gould had already ruffled many feathers in the party.

Mandelson left the party's employment with a view to fighting the Hartlepool seat at the general election. A number of shadow Cabinet members were incensed by his habit of promoting, at every opportunity, two comparative newcomers to the party's front rank, Gordon Brown and Tony Blair. For every individual Mandelson seemed to win over, there was always at least one whom he alienated.

I had known him when we both worked for the Labour Party. He was the very antithesis of my view of politics. To me, he was all froth and bubble. Mind you, he was very good at that type of thing, but he was alarmingly touchy about criticism. At one meeting at party headquarters in Walworth Road, he was furious at my comments about the launch of a health campaign. He stormed out of the meeting, completely misunderstanding my point. I did not give a damn – I had more important concerns than the hissy fits of Mandelson.

Gould, too, had faced his difficulties. The National Executive was disappointed enough in him to cut off funding for his polling activities. However, this did not stop him. Neil Kinnock then started to pay him using Short money, the allowance given to opposition parties to fund their leader's office. Gould, like Mandelson, was to make a dramatic return to centre stage before too long.

However, having been in opposition for thirteen years between 1951 and 1964, many Labour members just assumed that the 1992 election would be 'our turn' after another thirteen years of grinding opposition. Morale was high with a general expectation that, with one last heave, we would sail into government. How wrong we were. Once the campaign proper was under way, there were problems for all to see. We were not as well prepared as we thought in many of the seats we needed to win to form a government. True, there were to be successes, which brought the Tory majority right down from 102 to a mere twenty-one. It was an impressive result, but not good enough. The 'War of Jennifer's Ear' had been a disaster for Labour's campaign, when Robin Cook appeared at odds with a family over their daughter's medical condition. This was immeasurably worsened by the on-camera performance of a press officer intruding on a Neil Kinnock press conference. Neil's own American-style hootin' and hollerin' at a glitzy campaign event in Sheffield gave an impression of triumphalism. We had fluffed it.

After two shots at winning – and failing – the dream ticket had to go. Neil was bitterly disappointed. Shortly after the election defeat, he was very angry and he kicked a door in his Westminster office in pure frustration. He knew how close he had been to his greatest ambition and knew that he had blown it. We did not blame him – it was a collective failure of the Labour Party to recognise just how far the political landscape had altered under Mrs Thatcher. I, together with neighbouring members, took Neil and Glenys for a meal at a West End restaurant to cheer them up. I think that whilst Glenys was bitter about unnamed senior colleagues who were less than supportive of Neil, he himself was pleased by the stream of strangers who came across to commiserate with him.

For my money, there was a great deal of snobbery towards Neil – the Welsh 'boyo' as some papers described him. Years later, Scotsman Michael Martin was to face similar hostility as Speaker, being labelled 'Gorbals Mick'. It is evident in Parliament that if one attacks the rich and privileged it is 'class politics', to be condemned. However, it is perfectly acceptable, it seems, for 'commentators' like Quentin Letts and his ilk to disparage those who have been high achievers from humble origins. It is the snobbery of a section of the English establishment which I find so offensive and pointless.

With the resignation of Neil Kinnock and Roy Hattersley, a new leadership had to be elected. There was little doubt in my mind who the successful candidate would be. It would be John Smith, shadow Chancellor under Neil Kinnock. An Edinburgh lawyer by profession, John represented one of the two Monkland seats in Scotland, an area where religious sectarianism was rife. Yet John had repeatedly won the support of both Protestants and Catholics, such was his charm and integrity.

Not everyone saw him as Mr Nice Guy. There were some who insisted that he had despised Kinnock and constantly undermined him. I know of no evidence of that. Rather, I recall his visit with Kinnock to a Bolton engineering plant, Beloit Walmsley, when he was happy to trail unnoticed in the wake of a horde of photographers and journalists focused on Kinnock during a tour of the plant. I actually asked him during the tour whether he felt pushed out. He just smiled and said: 'Neil is the leader, and it is he who they want to hear.'

John's family continued to live in Edinburgh. Ironically, that meant that backbenchers saw more of him than either his predecessor or his successor. When his work was done, he could not slip off to his family home. He would often stay and have a whisky in the Smoking Room. Thus he was a familiar and respected figure to his colleagues, always both affable and accessible. He was a shoo-in as leader.

There was a challenger – the New Zealand academic Bryan Gould. Bryan presented himself as the representative of the Labour left, in contrast to John Smith's right credentials. My neighbour George Howarth had a telling story about Bryan, although he supported him on political grounds. George had been invited to dinner at Bryan's flat with Bryan's wife and daughter. Four places were set, three with linen napkins, one with a paper napkin. As George sat, Bryan's wife swapped the linen napkin before George with the paper one.

The real contest, if there was to be one, was for deputy leader. Bryan Gould threw his hat in the ring for that too, as did Margaret Beckett and John Prescott. Robin Cook was managing John Smith's campaign, and he telephoned me at home from his cottage in the New Forest. I assured him that John had my support; then he raised Margaret's name, and I told him in no uncertain terms that I could not support her. When he asked why, I replied that she had signed a minority report after the National Executive inquiry into the Militant Tendency in Liverpool. Anyone who had sought to exonerate Militant would get no support from me.

As it happened, I supported John Prescott. He did not win, as the party establishment swung behind Margaret, but I felt that the trade union wing of the party was still a weighty element in the coalition we call the Labour Party and deserved a high place at the table. Prescott was the only one of the three candidates to fit the bill.

Whilst this was going on, I received a telephone call from a woman named Anji Hunter. She had taken a job with Tony Blair and was ringing on his behalf. Would I like to join him for dinner one evening? When I raised the question of the venue, she said that they did not really know the places around Westminster. That was certainly true of Tony. His family lived in Islington. He did not hang around Westminster, but at every opportunity sped off to the family home. As a result, few in Westminster actually knew him – he didn't mix.

I had first met him during the Richmond by-election, which brought William Hague into Westminster. We were canvassing together in and around Catterick. He was irritated by the arrangement that had the canvassing team stop at a pub for lunch – then he discovered that the landlord was a Sedgefield constituent, and turned the charm on like a tap.

He had also campaigned in a local election battle with Militant in Liverpool. He came on the street in the Netherley ward with myself and the candidate, Barry Navarro. Several carloads of opponents ambushed us, yelling and screaming into our faces. Knowing that Tony had never experienced this type of political confrontation, I was taken with how calm he remained. He went into what I later thought of as meditation mode. That is, he had this knack of appearing to take himself outside the immediate fray, focusing on something far away. I was to see him do this regularly when he entered the Commons chamber to face a grilling, adopting an air of intense concentration, yet untrammelled by the fuss around him.

After we left the area by car, he asked how it was that dissident groups could use the word 'Labour' in their title with impunity. I reminded him that he was the lawyer, not I. Given the suggestion that he worked on the expulsion of Militant from Labour's ranks, I found his lack of awareness of this point very telling. Precisely what legal work had he done which left such culpable ignorance of the tactics of our internal enemy?

Still, he had conducted himself well in trying circumstances, and I gave him credit for that. I know his father-in-law, Tony Booth, who had long seen himself as a celebrity campaigner for Labour. I would never have put him and his son-in-law in the same family if I had not known of their relationship. Not having met Cherie at that stage, I wondered just what kind of a person could be the conduit between such dissimilar characters.

Anyway, I arranged to go with Tony to the Vitello d'Oro, a restaurant in the basement of Church House. It was an early sitting as I knew that Tony would want to get home handily. We were the only people in there, until Neil Kinnock arrived with his staff for a farewell meal – 'the Last Supper', I suggested to an unsmiling Tony. We ate and we talked without ever getting to the point – why Tony wanted to have a meal with me. With hindsight, I realise that I had unwittingly told Tony what he wanted to know when I recounted my telephone call from Robin Cook. He was, in my view, pondering whether he should have a go for the deputy's job. When I described the joint ticket, I believe he saw discretion as the better part of valour. Two years later, he was proven to have made the right call. Even if he had made the grade as deputy, two years in the job would have given ample scope to create enough enemies to halt any higher ambitions.

None of this occurred to me at the time. Instead, another facet of Tony Blair stuck with me. He did not like to be argued with. I had said that I believed a member should be part of the community he or she represented and live there. The man who had given his own selection conference the impression that he would live in Trimdon was quite exercised by this, using the old cliché 'I am elected to represent Sedgefield in Westminster, not Westminster in Sedgefield'. We agreed to disagree.

two

John Smith won the leadership contest overwhelmingly. On his coat tails, Margaret Beckett became deputy. Bryan Gould was to leave Parliament and return to his native New Zealand. The next time I saw him was in Shanghai, of all places. John Prescott, of course, remained to fight another day, having established himself as a party heavyweight to be reckoned with.

The new regime quickly established itself with a new leadership support team, led by a cerebral Scot, Murray Elder. John Smith had to deal with a party shattered by the 1992 election defeat. It was hard to believe that we had to face another Tory parliament after thirteen years of grinding opposition. Many new Labour members had entered in that election and were eager to push on to victory. However, even they were tempered in their enthusiasm by the task ahead. Those of us who had already experienced the thankless pain of opposition felt worse.

However, John's optimism and quiet good humour was a tonic. He immediately set about using what talents he felt were available to him within the Parliamentary Labour Party to reconstruct a fighting opposition, sensing the weakness of the Tory government under John Major. One 'talent' he did not call in was the newly elected member for Hartlepool, Peter Mandelson. John had little time for the presentational tricks of Mandelson and even less for his conspiratorial habits. As a result, Mandelson was an anonymous figure for the duration of John Smith's leadership.

To my pleasant surprise, I was called to the colours in the whips' office. There is no better place to learn how Parliament operates than from the perspective of that office. So arcane are the mysteries of parliamentary procedure, and so much hinges on that procedure, that a first job as a whip is a true apprenticeship in the workings of Parliament. I was very happy to do the job, whilst admitting my ignorance of the subtleties of the role. In fact, the very first time I conducted a vote it was a tremendous foul-up.

I and another whip, Alan Meale, were appointed tellers for a vote in the Commons. The procedure seems straightforward. The motion is put at the end of debate by the Speaker. Members shout 'Aye' or 'No'. Where there is a split – and there usually is – the Speaker calls 'Division' and members go into either the 'Aye' or the 'No' lobby to vote.

However, as members wander into the lobbies, the tellers – normally two government and two opposition whips – flank the Speaker, who reads out the names of the tellers before they go off to count the votes. On this occasion, on Alan Meale's instruction, I went to the exit of the 'No' lobby, as he went to the 'Aye' lobby.

It occurred to me – with some prompting – that some part of the process had been missed.

I went back to the Speaker's chair, but Alan was lost in the crowd at the door from the 'Aye' lobby. The Speaker, Betty Boothroyd, immediately declared the vote off, as the opposition had not appointed tellers. She would not change her mind even as Alan returned to join me at her side.

The debate had been a financial one and the responsibility of Gordon Brown. He went ballistic when our disagreement with the government on the issue could not be recorded by a vote. I dare say that, in my case, it simply added to an established dislike of me.

Our relationship had soured when I was a regional organiser for the Labour Party. In that role, I had responsibility for by-elections within my region, the north-west of England. Following the death of Alan Roberts, the member for Bootle, there was to be a by-election. The party had established a template for such trying events, which included a programme of visiting senior politicians plugging their particular briefs. Thus, if an education spokesman visited, we would build the day around the education theme. It would start with a press conference, followed by a visit to a school or college. There would be ever more ingenious adaptations of this, but the scheduled thematic approach was a constant.

In a given by-election, such visits were co-ordinated through the Parliamentary Labour Party. On one particular day, Gordon Brown was pencilled in. Advance briefing was done and arrangements made, but then Brown's chief of staff, Paul McKinney, telephoned the campaign headquarters to pull him out. We were furious, even more so when he was then rude to one of our press officers.

I took the phone from her and gave him a piece of my mind. If Brown did not show, I told him, I would take his place at the press conference, explaining to the fourth estate that Brown had not turned up. Next thing, Brown was on the telephone himself, full of his trademark hectoring. I told him his attempt at pulling out just would not wash, least of all with his parliamentary colleagues who were out on the knocker in the by-election. He came and, as I recall, it was an uneventful visit; but I am sure that he harboured a grudge.

Whilst in the whips' office, I worked with a rather jolly Scot named Tommy McAvoy, who told me his only ambition was to be a whip in government. Although he resigned as an opposition whip – because, he said, of the anti-Scottish views of the senior whips – he was to make that career in the Whips' Office, being a senior whip from 1 May 1997 to date. One of his colleagues was Gordon McMaster, the MP for Paisley, a tragic young man who was to commit suicide. The semi-detached whip from London was the late Tony Banks, who never took anything in Parliament too seriously.

It was a tremendous learning process, hindered only by the inadequacy of the whips' leadership. It was in the hands of Derek Foster, a Salvation Army bandsman from Bishop Auckland. He struck me as a nice but weak man. He had been shoe-horned into the job to get him out of Neil Kinnock's office, where he had been Neil's parliamentary private secretary. He was aided and abetted by a devious man called Ray Powell, the late member for Ogmore.

Powell was the man who traded votes in the election of the parliamentary committee for favours. He could do favours, too, for he was accommodation and pairing whip. If you wanted an office, you spoke to Ray Powell. If you needed time off the whip, you spoke to him. If you wanted to go abroad, you checked with him. In return, some members handed over their blank voting papers for the parliamentary committee. Thus he reinforced the position of those struggling to win by straight votes. In turn, they looked to him and supported him through the parliamentary committee.

It was a corrupt system, and one that would be even more damaging if we were to win power. I recall on one occasion, when Ron Davies had challenged Powell's position, asking Alistair Darling which way he would vote, hoping he would answer that he wanted to end the current corrupt regime. Instead Alistair told me that Powell had promised him a better office, so he would be assured of his vote, provided he came good. So much for the principled approach, I thought.

Matters were worse when it came to time off. Two people stood out in my mind as constantly seeking time off. One was Dr John Gilbert – now Lord Gilbert – who seemed to spend more time in the United States than in the United Kingdom when we were in opposition. The only time he sought to be involved was when we debated the Intelligence and Security Bill. I was the opposition whip responsible, and he was desperate, for some reason, to sit on the bill committee.

The other notable absentee was a rising star called Tony Blair. He may have had, as he constantly argued, a young family over in Islington, but many others had young families too. Unlike Blair, they were not constantly finding reasons why they had to leave early and miss votes.

The exception in the whips' office was Don Dixon, deputy chief whip and member for Jarrow. A former shipyard worker, he was the man who made the opposition machine tick. He had more political nous than half the shadow Cabinet put together. Why he was not chief whip I could not fathom. I put it down to a lack of confidence for the top job, although he was head and shoulders over Foster. Besides, he had the real power whilst the at-times hapless Foster took the responsibility.

I became the whip for two departments – the Foreign Office and the new 'Ministry of Fun', the Department for National Heritage, run by the thoroughly dislikeable David Mellor. Unfortunately, my two departmental teams initially met at the same time, and I found myself missing one or other of the meetings. Not that it mattered much. I did not find them too impressive.

Mo Mowlam ran National Heritage, taking over from Ann Clwyd. Whilst the latter flew into rages with her staff – one came to work for me after falling foul of Ann – Mo directed her ire at her two juniors , Robin Corbett and Tom Pendry, now both in the Lords. So lacking in diligence were these two that on one occasion, during the National Lotteries Bill, they both cried off ill. I, as whip, was left to argue their amendments in committee. Strangely, they both managed to keep lunch engagements that day.

Jack Cunningham took over the Foreign Office from Robin Cook. His arrogant conceit knew no bounds. He patronised just about everybody whilst seeming to do very little. Meetings consisted of Jack saying how wonderful he was, whilst the rest of us had to wait our turn for something constructive to emerge. John Smith's foreign policy adviser, Meta Ramsay (now, like Jack, in the Lords), would quietly sit, sometimes knitting like a latter-day Madame Defarge, saying little but taking it all in. I would love to have been a fly on the wall when she reported back to John Smith, her old friend.

There were many things to dislike about Jack, although I well recall defending him against Militant abuse in Liverpool. The first time I took exception to his behaviour was when he turned on his devoted supporter Roger Stott, then the member for Wigan. Roger did not reciprocate, and Jack seemed intent on mocking the almost innocent Roger. On another occasion, whilst running a by-election where the absent Jack was nominally the campaign co-ordinator,

I received a telephone call from him at campaign headquarters at 9.00 on a Sunday evening. He was very surprised at finding me on duty. This, of course, begs the question why he had telephoned me then on my direct line. Perhaps he was hoping that I would not be there and was planning to make an issue of it. I just do not know.

When the annual beauty contest of elections for the parliamentary committee came around, John Spellar, the hard right member for Warley, attended one of our departmental meetings. It turned into a campaign meeting for Jack. To their anger, I said that I did not wish to be involved in campaigning for that election. Spellar immediately accused me of having agreed to have done just that for David Blunkett. I was appalled. I was being charged with hypocrisy, yet it was not true. I do not know what Blunkett had said to Spellar. I recalled saying to Blunkett I would vote for him, not work for him – a very different proposition.

Unfortunately, that was – and remains – the position in the PLP. Cliques form, with a leading political light surrounded by acolytes. The latter go out to persuade others to vote for their man or woman. Sometimes, deals are done to 'swap' votes – that is, to persuade 'our' people to vote for 'your' candidate, if the favour is returned.

It really annoys me how members were prepared to debase themselves in the interests of their patron. The theory is that we are all honourable members; the reality is that some members are far more equal than the rest. Many believe that being a runner or bag-carrier for a politically prominent member is the way to promotion up that elusive greasy pole of ambition. In fact, for many, it has been so, and will remain so as long as everyone, from party leaders down, encourages cronyism.

Such behaviour begins early in a parliamentary career. I vividly recall the 1992 elections for the parliamentary committee. Harriet

Harman was making her annual visit to the Strangers' Bar in search of votes. She was accompanied by an acolyte, the newly elected Tessa Jowell. Her eyes fell upon the member for Motherwell, John Reid, who was a heavy drinker in those days. 'Would you like a drink, John?' she asked.

'No, Harriet, I don't want your drink; but see wee Dougie Henderson there? He likes posh tarts like you.'

Unabashed, Harriet swivelled on her heels and said: 'Dougie, can I buy you a drink?' So much for a sophisticated electorate.

This type of activity repeated itself across the bars and tearooms of Westminster, in the hope that a place on the parliamentary committee would lead eventually to a place in a Labour Cabinet, as convention dictated. Yet it was highly divisive as supporters built up the profile of their candidates whilst simultaneously discrediting others seeking a place in the parliamentary sun. All of the time, Ray Powell loitered in the shadows with a fistful of votes to sway the results.

The result of this was predictable: inadequate individuals – or just lazy ones – in critical leading positions in the fight for parliamentary dominance, and it was a fight. Although the Tories had won the 1992 election with a working majority, it was a small one which over time could be eroded by attritional political warfare. The Labour opposition benefited from the calamitous and precipitous withdrawal from the European exchange rate mechanism in September 1992. Major's fledgling new government was never to recover from that extremely costly national setback. Nevertheless, John Smith would need a solid team behind him to wear down the Tories and secure victory at the next election.

Of course, he could not always get his way. I like to think that Labour is still a democratic party. When a vacancy occurred on the parliamentary committee, George Robertson put himself forward with Smith's support. I could not support him and told George so. I felt that we had far too many Scots in the shadow Cabinet, and needed to persuade the English of the virtues of a putative Labour government. George – and a number of other Scots – were less than happy with my argument.

This was not unusual in itself. The northern English regions had long argued that the Scots – and, to a lesser degree, the Welsh – were benefited to our disadvantage by the Barnett formula. This gave the Scots extra funding to dampen the demand for devolution. As they received that money, northern England was further squeezed by a mechanism called the area cost adjustment. This sliced off about a billion pounds from northern local authorities to subsidise the 'more expensive' south-east. It is hardly surprising that tensions grew over much political and financial squeezing.

My office at this time was a prefabricated structure on one of Westminster's roofs. Powell had never seen fit to ensure that I had any kind of office, until I literally forced the issue with him. As a member of the Whips' Office, even I had to be given something, although there were people still housed in what was known as the Cloisters. These were literally closed-off corridors with desks in, providing some space for members, although totally inadequate. It was viewed by many as a form of political Siberia. Thus Ken Livingstone was put there for the duration of his parliamentary career.

Mind you, I personally had few worries about my office and its low status. Such matters were of little consequence to me, especially as I had a second desk in the Whips' Office, just off the Members' Lobby. We would meet there each day to discuss the handling of the day's business and raise any pertinent matters. It was often a little strained because it was chaired by Derek Foster; yet we looked to

Don Dixon for real leadership. Embarrassingly, if it was a whip's birthday, Foster and his wife would produce fruit juice and a little birthday cake. We would be expected to sing 'Happy Birthday' to the unfortunate individual and make merry as if at a children's party.

There remained important business. The Tories were fractured over Europe, and we had to widen the gap at every opportunity. That required good organisation and the sensible use of time. The latter cannot be overstated. The Tories were in government. That meant ministers being kept for votes late into the night – sometimes all night. Those ministers still had red boxes to do and departments to run. It was guerrilla warfare in Parliament.

We would organise shifts to keep things going. It might be women members in one, trade unionists in another, London members on yet another, followed by the Scottish contingent. We would joke about the Lancashire Fusiliers standing ready, or the Scots Guards. John Smith was up for the battle and so were we.

Whilst this was the parliamentary scene, there were other issues affecting Labour. For example, there were the thorny questions of women's representation and of the trade unions' relations to the party. Regarding the gender imbalance, fierce arguments were going on about quotas. There were calls for ethnic quotas, also. Although more women came into Parliament in 1992, there was a long way to go.

The trade union issue was more ideological. There were those who, frankly, wanted trade unions out of the party, denying their historic role in the birth and development of the Labour Party. There were others who wanted to carry on with the block vote and union funding on a grand scale. What was needed was a more balanced approach to both, and John Smith provided a lead.

What we could not resile from was the changing nature of the electorate and of our electoral culture. Unions were losing members, and women were striving to break through the glass ceiling in many areas of life. It was impossible to avoid the conclusion that the Labour Party had to adapt to the new realities of our multicultural, post-industrial society in which expectations had radically altered. John Smith was aware of this, but was cautious by nature. He was not one to plunge recklessly into change for its own sake. The mentality that promoted permanent revolution was not one which he found attractive in any way. He was a man of compromise, rather than confrontation.

That did not mean he would not be tough if the situation demanded it. On one occasion Gerry Bermingham, a member for St Helens South, burst into the Strangers' Bar in a very agitated state. He was pursued by a very belligerent and drunk John Reid, who wished to do Gerry some physical harm for a perceived insult in the then nearby Annie's Bar. Gordon McMaster and I restrained John, got him a taxi and sent him home. We had done our duty as whips.

Apparently, on the following day John Smith sent for Reid and gave him an ultimatum: give up the drink, or there would be no future for him in the Labour Party. He meant it, and John Reid knew he meant it. To John Reid's credit, he did literally give up alcohol instantly. It showed the willpower of the ex-Communist that he was. Years later, he was to reinforce this image of a will of iron when, upon being appointed to the Department of Health, he similarly gave up cigarettes instantly, despite having been a heavy smoker all of his life.

John Smith also had an impish sense of humour. On one occasion, he mischievously wound up the unintelligible Tommy Graham, suggesting there was a role for him in a future John Smith government. Tommy took John's jest seriously, and it was some time before he could be persuaded that he was not destined for high office.

Recognising that elections are not just won in Westminster, John needed to be out and about in the country, selling the Labour prospectus. He felt that he was fit for exhausting forays around the country. After all, he was well on the way to climbing all of the Munros – these challenging mountain peaks of a certain height which were later to claim Robin Cook.

Thus it was the case that he went on yet another national tour in the spring of 1994. One of his stops was on Merseyside where a visit to a St Helens Labour social club was on the itinerary. He showed his political mettle by getting behind the bar, serving pints to the locals. Uniquely, they even halted the crowded bingo so that John could say a few words. The cheers for him rattled the rafters.

I drove him back to his hotel in Liverpool, together with my wife Bernadette. Although he must have been exhausted, he insisted that we stop for a while and gallantly poured my wife a glass of wine as a nightcap. As we bade him farewell, we did not realise that we would not speak with him again.

three

I was having breakfast in my flat when the telephone rang. It was a distraught Ian McCartney telling me that John had died of a heart attack within the last couple of hours. Like everyone else, I was stunned by the news. I quickly readied myself for the House and was there before 10.30 a.m.

The atmosphere in Westminster was like nothing I had known. I saw members literally in tears – and not just Labour ones. John Smith had been incredibly liked and respected by many people in all parties. It showed that day as the normally busy House ground to a halt.

Oddly, there were some people who, in an uncanny forerunner to the reaction to the death three years later of Princess Diana, were literally hysterical at the news of John's death. Individuals who had not been particularly close to him performed tears on camera outside Parliament, sharing their grief with a stunned and confused British public. In their case, never had so many cried so publicly with so little honesty.

Needless to say, there were more sanguine figures in the parliamentary shadows, already busying themselves with telephone calls to journalists as to who John's likely successor might be, whilst John's body was still resistant to the cold indifference of rigor mortis. Such is the way of politics in the eyes of some – the king (or, in this case, the leader) is dead; long live the king. This manoeuvring was the province of a tiny minority, not of the wider body of people which makes up Parliament. The latter reflect the people at large, unconsumed by the ambition that sees in a tragic premature death an opportunity rather than a loss. Whilst most of us mourned, there were, sadly, those who schemed and manipulated. What, I wonder, is so important in politics that such people should have such scant regard for human loss? It was a question which would come back to haunt me in the years to come.

In the days following John's death, but before his burial, the enormity of the political loss began to dawn on the Labour Party collectively. After the disappointment of the 1992 election, most of us had subscribed to the 'one last heave' theory. That is, with one increased effort behind John as leader, it would be Labour's 'turn' at the next election. John's death deprived us of his leadership, and many in the Parliamentary Labour Party began to believe we were almost cursed to electoral defeat. Behind that was a deeper fear – that defeat at the next election would be the end of the Labour Party as a political force.

The National Executive had another preoccupation. We were headed towards European parliamentary elections. A leadership contest during those elections would have a cataclysmic effect on the outcome, it was believed. Therefore it placed a moratorium on campaigning for the leadership until after those Euro-elections. In the interim, Margaret Beckett, as the elected deputy leader, would be the leader of the party pro tem.

John Smith's funeral was one of those occasions when the British obsession for pomp and ritual came into its own. It was covered live on television, as the political great and good joined John's family in Edinburgh for the funeral service. After that sombre event on the Friday, John's remains were transported to the island of Iona for final interment on the Saturday.

Like many others, I followed the service from afar – in my case, my home. I was there on that Saturday evening when the telephone rang. I took the call, from Tony Blair. He quickly came to the point. He would be putting himself forward for the leadership and wanted my help in organising his bid. I was not expecting such a conversation on that evening and mumbled something about having visitors – I would need to ring him the following morning. Frankly, I wanted time to think, and I did.

Who were to be the likely runners and riders in this race? Beckett, yes; Brown, of course; and probably Cook and Prescott, although I was not too sure if they would seek the job. Looking at the list, I saw no alternative. I believed that we needed an English leader, following two Celts, if we were to capture the fabled 'Middle England' for Labour. I did not believe either Beckett or Prescott had what it takes. Blair? To me – and the vast majority of Labour members, including in Parliament – he was a presentable and photogenic blank sheet, with one soundbite to his name – 'tough on crime, tough on the causes of crime'. Mistakenly, I believed he could be moulded.

There was one other issue. He and Brown were reputedly very close to Mandelson, a man cast aside by John Smith. When I rang him back on the Sunday morning, I told him that I was in, as long as Mandelson was not part of any campaign. Although I cannot recall Blair's words, he led me to believe that Mandelson had nothing to do with his campaign. This characteristic of giving the impression of saying one thing whilst later denying it was to become a hallmark of Blair.

He told me that he had also spoken with Mo Mowlam. After having arranged to meet him in his office the following morning, I rang off and then immediately telephoned Mo to compare notes. She told me that she, too, had signed up as long as Mandelson was out. Blair had assured her that was the case.

Thus, the nucleus of Blair's campaign team – or so we thought – met for the first time in 1 Parliament Street. It consisted of Tony Blair, his personal assistant, Anji Hunter, Mo Mowlam and myself. The first thing we needed to do was to rustle up some more people to start a surreptitious nomination campaign. This was vital if we were to develop an unstoppable momentum towards victory. Blair brought in Alun Michael, a member of his shadow Home Office team. Mo brought in Adam Ingram, but he did not return, having other demands on his time, she reported. Kevin Barron fleetingly appeared in that first week and then fell away. Only John McFall, a Scottish member, stayed the course.

Our first objective was to sign people up to the Blair candidacy, and I began on that first Monday. It needed to be done quickly and discreetly, given the moratorium on campaigning. What fascinated me was to see members of Brown's circle – Nick Brown, Martin O'Neill, Doug Henderson, Geoffrey Robinson – sounding out people's opinions as we were actually signing up members as nominators. This strategy was based on the belief that where the Parliamentary Labour Party went, the rest of the Labour movement would more or less follow.

On the Tuesday, Blair announced to his 'team' that he was going to establish a formal campaign committee. The question was: who would chair it? I quietly suggested Mo, but he was wholly unenthusiastic. He seemed to see Mo's role as delivering the women's vote. He then suggested Jack Straw. The next day, Jack looked into Blair's office when we were gathered there. He made one or two inconsequential remarks and then left. I had the impression that he was weighing up the strength of Team Blair. Moreover, I had reason to believe that he wanted to keep his own options open, in case an opportunity occurred for his own advancement.

He was not alone. At one stage, Jack Cunningham stopped me in the tearoom and told me that he had been encouraged to throw his hat into the ring. I gather he was testing the water for a bid. I laughed and told him to forget it. He seemed rather miffed at my dismissal of his chances.

There were other curiosities. My function was to deliver the nominations of members of Parliament. I kept a chart of who was supportive and who was not so keen. The very first to commit himself to Blair was Chris Smith. Others were not even approached, on the basis that they were firmly in another's camp. Thus, Clare Short was backing Beckett; Dick Caborn was running Prescott's campaign and Nick Brown was a long-standing acolyte of Gordon Brown. The last member of the shadow Cabinet to commit was Harriet Harman. I could never decide whether she believed a call might come for her to stand, or, more likely, she wanted to ensure that she was on the winning side.

These were very long and frantic days of piling up nomination promises, so that, by the first weekend, we could 'leak' a list of over half of the members of the PLP who were committed to Tony Blair. One interesting figure was the chief whip, Derek Foster, a constituency neighbour of Blair's. I suggested to Tony that he speak to Foster about his nomination. His report back was that Foster felt he must remain neutral in the succession battle. However, after seeing the leaked nominations list, he contacted the *Guardian* to say that his name had been missed off Tony's list of committee supporters! Everyone loves a winner.

Gordon Brown knew that he had been beaten to the draw. He appeared to be sulking, although he was reportedly in some sort of contact with Blair. Meanwhile, Prescott and Beckett saw themselves in the race for both the leadership and the deputy leadership. I saw logic in Prescott as deputy. He would be more representative of the wider Labour movement – an alien place for Blair. To that end, during the mornings I met on occasion with Ian McCartney of Prescott's team in the empty Smoking Room. Our joint aim was to get Prescott as Blair's running mate.

Blair himself was none too sure of this. What he quite had in mind he never really disclosed, but his initial reluctance to team up with Prescott was obvious. This may just have been the uncertainty of the novice – and he was a novice. For example, he stopped me in the Members' Lobby and asked my opinion of all-women shortlists (there was a controversial application of this at the time, in a Leeds constituency). I truthfully said that I did not like the idea, but could think of no other way to increase the number of women members.

He agreed, at least, that he did not like the idea; and he declared he was going to announce his view to the national women's conference the following Sunday! This was not smart electoral politics. I reported this conversation the following day at the campaign committee meeting, and the collective good sense of the committee on the issue dissuaded Blair from mentioning it on the hustings at that conference.

The campaign committee had now become established. Jack Straw chaired it. Barry Cox, an old friend of Tony, became the treasurer and head of fundraising. Anji Hunter represented Tony; Andrew Smith came on board, to represent Gordon's interest. Alun Michael sought to be on it, and Mo and I were the remaining members. It was not a formal committee, more a discussion group of allegedly like-minded people. Except we were not.

Almost immediately Jack Straw wanted to move beyond the election of a new leader to the dismantling of party policy. A former shadow Education Secretary, he began by seeking to change huge chunks of his successor Anne Taylor's flagship White Paper, *Opening Doors to a Learning Society*. I wanted nothing to do with this. I had signed up to ensure an electorally acceptable leader was well in place before the next election. It was not our role to destroy party policy without reference to the Labour movement. Some of my colleagues appeared to be planning an internal revolution by stealth. As a result, I began to stay away from any meetings, or part of them, other than those directly related to the leadership election campaign.

Regardless of these difficulties, Blair's campaign ran relatively smoothly, as it moved beyond Westminster and into the country. His trip to the north-west was an early foray into unknown territory. I met him, together with Anji Hunter, for his visit to the women's conference in Southport. En route, we had arranged a campaign event at a Labour club in St Helens.

It went well enough, with introductions from the two local members of Parliament, John Evans and Gerry Bermingham. Blair spoke well, of course, but he looked distinctly uneasy in the pressing tactile throng which besieged him as he left. As we left in the car, he actually said how offputting he found the affectionate greetings of the women members. The main course was to come, at Southport.

He already had a vision of himself and his future. To this end, in the car were Anji Hunter and Tim Allan, a staff member, plus a BBC journalist, Jon Sopel, who was to write a quick biography of Blair. I was later to describe this as hagiographic in a review I wrote. It was certainly inferior to another, more considered, biography, authored by John Rentoul.

Our little band made its way in my old Mondeo to Southport. Blair – who had a Volkswagen Beetle in those days – and Anji Hunter had been amused by my old car, which I had collected them in from the airport. I pointed out that he should not present himself as too flash in these Labour heartlands, and a posher car might not have gone down too well.

The conference had adjusted its format to incorporate leadership hustings in the afternoon session. Prescott, Beckett and Blair all addressed the conference. It seemed as if Beckett was less than enthusiastic in her speech, whilst Prescott was – well, Prescott, with mangled syntax. Blair himself, whilst fluent, was not at his best and resisted the temptation to denounce all-women shortlists.

As we left, his father-in-law, Tony Booth, appeared with his then wife, a Canadian lady, with their infant son. Blair appeared very uncomfortable with them, and whilst he was perfectly civil, his body language and urgent wish to leave the conference told a tale.

Leaving the conference, his preoccupation was in finding a church en route to Manchester where he could attend Sunday service. Driving along the M58, I spotted a spire and headed for the parish church of the village of Bickerstaffe. We arrived just in time for evensong. I asked Tony if he would like me to accompany him in, but he declined. He did, however, ask for some money for the collection.

Whilst he prayed, the rest of us loitered. I was interested to see two gravestones adjacent to each other in the names of Bickerstaffe and Prescot. Rodney and John were friends, and I made some light-hearted joke about the graves. Being a journalist, Jon Sopel was later to put a different, less humorous spin on my account, which caused me some embarrassment with the very-much-alive R. Bickerstaffe and J. Prescott.

Meanwhile, in the church, the astonished vicar and his small number of worshippers struggled through the liturgy in the company of their unexpected and celebrated co-religionist. I often wonder what they really thought of this introduction to New Labour made flesh.

As I had always believed, the result was in no doubt. Blair was elected leader and Prescott became his deputy. The coronation took place in glorious weather at the London Institute of Education. I had been allocated a front row seat, but chose to linger at the back of the hall with my friend Fraser Kemp. I had little interest in the reflected glory of the nascent Sun King of New Labour. I just wanted a Labour government.

Two receptions followed, one for Blair at Church House and another for Prescott on a ship moored at Westminster, known mischievously as 'the ship of shame'. I went first to Church House. When I saw Blair, he was talking to his constituency neighbour, Stuart Bell. He greeted me and said, no doubt sincerely: 'I will never forget what you have done for me.' I made some weak joke in response and the hubbub of conversation and congratulations resumed. It was some time later that a journalist asked me who 'Bobby' was. I told him, truthfully, that I did not have a clue to whom or what he was referring. He then explained that on the balcony outside the reception, Blair had extended special thanks in an impromptu speech to 'Bobby'.

I did not know what this meant; nor did I dwell on it. Shortly after, I made my way to Prescott's bash, to toast his success. It was there that it was suggested that 'Bobby' was a reference to Mandelson. I did not know what the truth was, but it was disturbing. In fact, I went back to my flat rather than to a private party being thrown for Blair and his inner circle at the home of one of his wealthy friends in Putney. Once home, I made a few calls and was satisfied that the reference was indeed to Mandelson, who had been secretly in liaison with Blair throughout the leadership campaign. No doubt, in line with his usual practice, Mandelson was claiming credit for its success to his media friends, gullible as they were.

I bit my lip and decided to sleep on it before deciding what, if anything, to do or say. The following morning, I rang the Blair household and spoke to our new leader. I asked him directly why he had lied to me at the outset about Mandelson's involvement. Tellingly, he did not deny his lie; he just mumbled that Mandelson could get to papers no one else could reach. I saw no justification in that and said so. I asked him how he could mislead Mo Mowlam and myself on that. I received no satisfactory answer, just a failed attempt to jolly me up. That lie was to be the leitmotif of my attitude to Blair from then on.

It was not just Mo and I. If it was, perhaps the need to win was so overpowering that a failure of judgement, as over Mandelson's role, was understandable and forgivable; but there were other instances. One involved the chief whip, Derek Foster.

I had long said that the whips' office was unfit for Labour in office. I, therefore, liaised with Dick Caborn about standing against Foster's re-election. We were both candidates. Blair asked me if I could win – although newly elected leader, he was very unsure of himself in the role. I replied that it was highly unlikely that either I or Dick could win against the powerful patronage advantages of the incumbent. I did feel, however, that we could destabilise the regime, enabling the leader to force through change. Blair was uncomprehending of a strategy like that. In his highly personal approach to politics, he would only enter for what he personally could win.

It turned out that Dick and I combined were eleven votes short of turning out the chief whip, but the writing was on the wall. Some weeks later, at the weekly PLP meeting, Blair announced that the chief whip was standing down and handed the floor to Foster. The latter gracefully fell on his sword and then dropped a bombshell. The leader, he announced, had promised him a place in his first Cabinet. Prescott was thunderstruck and Blair adopted a look of surprise.

Later, Blair was to say that he did not know why Foster had drawn that conclusion. However, it was to be a regular occurrence that people believed they had an assurance from Blair, only for him to claim something entirely different. Oddly, when he came into office, Derek Foster was the shortest office holder in Blair's first government. He was given a job, not in the Cabinet, but in the Cabinet Office. He was appointed on Saturday 3 May and resigned on Sunday 4 May, from Blackpool, where he was attending a Salvation Army event.

This early common 'misreading' by others of their conversations with Blair was complemented by his discomfort in his new role as leader. There was a tension in him. On the one hand, he was impatient to make progress and irritated by any resistance or disagreement with what he said or wanted. On the other hand, he was smart enough to know that he was an unknown quantity to most of those who had voted him in as Labour leader. That was obvious to me when I was collecting nominees in the leadership contest. There were those who simply wanted to back the eventual winner. Others saw a right-wing soul mate. Yet more were unwilling to support Prescott or Beckett – or even the undeclared Brown and Cook. He was a blank sheet to most – or, increasingly, all things to all men and women.

Nowhere was this more evident than with provincial, working class trade union members, whose favourite watering hole in Westminster was the Strangers' Bar, nicknamed the Kremlin by the Tories. I believed that it was as good a place as any for the new leader to impress his socialist Praetorian guard. He made an appearance along with his new parliamentary private secretary, Bruce Grocott. He had chosen well in Bruce, an immensely likeable man, who had been my campaign manager in the by-election which had initially brought me into Parliament.

When he arrived, I had ready a circle of hard-nosed, cynical 'brothers' who wanted to seriously size up the new man. It was a measure of how detached Blair had always been that none of them had ever had a conversation with him, although they were his contemporaries in Parliament. He was not a Commons man; he had always dashed off home for the pleasures of family life and his own social circle.

I asked our two 'visitors' what they would like to drink. Bruce quickly answered: 'A pint of bitter,' then his boss asked for a soda water, until a nudge from Bruce solicited a change in order to 'a half, please'. The lads in the bar weighed up his artifice quickly, but Blair decided to show his 'knowledge' of the Strangers' by asking after Ted, its head barman. Unfortunately, the memorable Ted had retired some years before. Blair compounded the poor image he was making by speaking of the types of beer tap used in the Strangers'. They too, like Ted, had departed some years before. He simply illustrated that he had little in common with that section of the Parliamentary Labour Party, not having shared their company in the Strangers' for some years.

They were a warm, friendly, gregarious bunch who liked nothing better in their own time than to have a beer and a sing-song. They were of a time and a place alien to Blair, although he learnt to ham it up in such company for the cameras. It was always a pose, and that was regrettable. Here was the heart and soul of the Labour movement, its parliamentary frontline. When we needed to fight attritionally night after night, they were the people who kept the debates going and provided the necessary votes. When there was a by-election – and there were quite a few – they were the campaigning shock troops prepared to go anywhere in the country for the Labour cause.

Sadly, for many of them, still loyal, but realising that their personal careers were ending, Blair was not a leader with whom they could identify. They looked forward to a well-earned retirement. Others believed that they still had a role to play in the Commons. In the middle there were those already looking to trade their safe Labour seat for a peerage. None of this was of any consequence to the leader. He had his eyes on higher things. After all, he wanted the Labour Party as a platform for his highly personal ambitions.

four

Once elected leader, Blair began to display those characteristic contradictions which were his hallmark. I quickly learnt that he could hold two mutually exclusive propositions as true at the same time. It was about whatever suited him at any given moment. This bipolarity was reflected in his early tentative attempts both to assert himself and to avoid any ruptures with the Labour Party. This was understandable enough for any new leader, particularly one who was so cautiously detached from – and even ideologically indifferent to – his own party.

Thus, his bargaining with Derek Foster over the job of chief whip, and his foray into the Strangers' Bar, were signs of him feeling his way into the role. He knew that the job carried great authority; he just did not know initially how to exercise that authority. What he did know – and was presumably being advised by his familiars like Peter Mandelson and Philip Gould – was that he wanted to make big personnel changes and to set up his own personal team of key advisers.

He put together his leader's office with audacity. Anji Hunter was a stalwart who was to become gatekeeper in the office. This was key. No one got past Anji unless she agreed it. To the surprise of everyone, he appointed Jonathan Powell as his chief of staff. Jonathan's brother Charles had been a key adviser to Mrs Thatcher in Downing Street. Apparently Blair had met Jonathan when he was a diplomat in our Washington embassy and was impressed by him. Presumably the regard was mutual, as Jonathan agreed to leave the diplomatic corps and head up Blair's office.

He was tougher than he looked. Soon after he began, he came for a drink with me. I introduced him to Laurence Cunliffe, an MP from an mining background, who was not slow in coming forward to tell Jonathan what he thought of 'people like him' in words of one syllable. Jonathan gave back as good as he got, which, I believe, rather pleased Laurence.

Another key appointment was that of head of policy. The appointee was the son of the renowned academic Ralph Miliband, David. Tall, dark and somewhat otherworldly, there was no doubting David's intellectual ability. However, he did not appear to be too knowledgeable about either the ways of the world or politics. Only time would tell if he would oversee policy development that was practical rather than theoretical. I took David on a tour of the Palace of Westminster and he was clearly in awe of the place – except, that is, in the Strangers' Bar, where he settled for an orange juice rather than a beer.

Yet probably the most public, and in some ways controversial, appointment was that of Alastair Campbell as Blair's spokesman.

Much has been written about Alastair – his loyalty to Robert Maxwell, his past drink problems – but I knew him as a good lobby journalist for the *Daily Mirror* and a Labour supporter.

In fact, I had appeared as a defence witness for him and his colleague David Bradshaw (later Blair's speechwriter) in a libel case brought by Tory MP Rupert Allason. The latter had won over twenty libel actions in succession, so it was a relief for Alastair and David to be exonerated at the Old Bailey. I like to think that they were grateful for my small contribution on their behalf.

Alastair was – and is – a forthright man. Over time, it appeared that he was telling Blair what to do and say, rather than the other way around. As such, he became central to much of the satire and parody that became fashionable in entertainment circles during the Blair years. What was incontrovertible, however, was that he understood the media better than anyone in a similar role had ever done. Joe Haines and Bernard Ingham had had their day, but Alastair was to develop into much more than the Prime Minister's spokesman. He was to determine the strategy for all presentational issues across the government.

This was the core of his team, backed up by a second echelon, including Kate Garvey and Tim Allan. In due course, these were to be supplemented by others whose importance was inversely proportionate to the claims they made for themselves. There were two other ever-presents who were, however, to have such influence on Blair as to substitute style and presentation for substance. They were Peter Mandelson and Philip Gould.

Mandelson's comeback under Blair after his marginalisation by John Smith was quite a feat, to be repeated almost ad nauseam in successive administrations. As Smith had blackballed Mandelson, the National Executive's Finance and General Purposes Committee had turned the tap off on funding Gould's polling for the party. Luckily for him, Neil Kinnock had used Short money (parliamentary funding for the office of the leader of the opposition) to carry on paying his way. Thus, these two had a lot to be grateful for in the election of Tony Blair as leader of the Labour Party. It would not be long before their shallow approach to the Labour Party's values was to be displayed.

The first meeting of the shadow front bench was held in the Commons in the Lower Ministerial Meeting Room. We were all keen and eager to hear the new leader set out his ideas for the march towards electoral success and government. I was dismayed to hear from his gurus Mandelson and Gould about a 'Clintonian' approach to the next election. It was dismissive of loyal Labour voters.

When I questioned this, Gould answered that 'they have nowhere else to go but Labour'. Quite apart from the arrogance and vacuity of such a view, I pointed to Australia where the blue-collar vote had recently swung over to the racist, xenophobic Pauline Hanson, after being taken for granted by the Australian Labor Party (ALP). An Australian friend, Wayne Swan (now Federal Treasurer), had told me that as the ALP had targeted new groups of Labor-friendly voters, traditional voters were falling away. However, the uncomfortable Australian example was not to be seriously considered. The triangulation of Clinton was the way forward for New Labour.

This adoption of the adjective 'New' was another marketing ploy. No one outside the leader's intimates was ever asked about the change. Rather, most people in the Labour movement insisted on ignoring the 'New' label. Our party remained, for most of us, simply 'the Labour Party'. In fact, I know of no one who was ever elected as 'New' Labour – only as 'the Labour Party candidate.'

Mandelson's own insipid vision of what politics should be about was to be set out in *The Blair Revolution*, co-authored by Roger Liddle, a deserter to the SDP who was to be rewarded with an adviser's job in Downing Street. This trite 'work' was a cause of great amusement in Labour Party circles. I wrote a highly critical review of it in *Tribune* and found myself being congratulated simultaneously by Tony Benn and Roy Hattersley! A rare conjunction of views.

Blair called me into his office after the review, on some pretext or other. What he really wanted was to find out if there was something else behind my criticism. I pointed out to him that, in the foreword, the authors had asserted that the book bore 'no one's imprimatur other than our own' and that I had repeated that with relief in the opening lines of my critique. He seemed happy to accept that.

However, he had not been happy with party management, either within the Commons or in the country as a whole. As a result Larry Whitty was to be kicked upstairs to the House of Lords and Tom Sawyer of the National Union of Public Employees, and on the soft left of the Labour Party, was to take his place.

Replacing the chief whip had been straightforward, with Donald Dewar now in the role; the real difficulty was the post of deputy. It had already been worked out that in a Labour government, Dewar would be Secretary of State for Scotland, charged with bringing forward devolution. Therefore, the role of deputy was viewed as an apprenticeship for the eventual chief whip in government. For two days, there was debate about this. The retiring deputy chief whip, Don Dixon, wanted me in the role. I suspect that Blair did too, but he would not show his hand. Dewar was dead set against it and, supported by Gordon Brown, wanted Nick Brown to have it.

There were a number of issues here. Firstly, Gordon Brown 'looked after' his people, those who had supported him, whereas Blair would trade off his own granny for a tactical advantage. Dewar was a Brown supporter, not least because of Blair's close friendship with Derry Irvine, for whom Dewar's wife had left him. Nick Brown was the most faithful of Brownites.

On the other hand, I was seen as a Blairite, not to be trusted in a key job like chief whip. Gordon Brown, after all, had already started his long campaign to replace Blair and take what he thought was his rightful role as Labour Party leader. Additionally, Don Dixon had issues with Nick Brown within his own north-eastern region and within the GMB union. Nor was he known as a lover of Scots.

The result was that Gordon Brown, through Donald Dewar, got his way. I expected such an attitude from Brown. As for Dewar, I saw him as a snob. Scots MPs alleged that he was religiously sectarian, but I had no personal experience of that. It was, after all, a large element in Scottish politics. The only real sectarianism in English Labour Party politics was ideological, not religious.

It was round about this time that I had urged Tony Blair not to forget the poor when he was elected Prime Minister. He replied that he knew all about the poor. I questioned this, given his own background. One example: he had told me that his father had once bid for Shincliffe Hall, a large former sanatorium where I had lodged as a student at Durham University. No one able to bid for such a pile, set in its own grounds, could be described as poor. He said that I misunderstood – that he had learnt of poverty through Cherie.

'How was that?' I asked.

He replied: 'Do you know she had to share a bed with her sister?'

I told him that in my own home, there were five in a bed and my Uncle Willie in the same room. The look of horror on his faced, mixed with incredulity, was a wonder to behold. What he did not grasp was that we were children at the time, not the weighty adults of later years. His naivety was almost endearing.

Of course, having his team and his party geared up for action was important, but so was support from the media. From the start of his campaign for the leadership, he had been conscious of the importance of presenting the right image. This was no doubt in part down to Mandelson's influence.

A very good example was a visit to Liverpool Football Club. I went to collect him and his family from the home of a family friend in the city. When I arrived, Tony had on a black suit with a black polo-neck sweater. He looked more like an Apache dancer than the leader of a political party. His wife had on a huge baggy sweater and multi-coloured leggings. I pointed out that the local great and good turned out for the lunch at the club in best bib and tucker. He listened intently and then left the room to make a call, presumably to Mandelson. After the call, he quickly changed into a white shirt and tie, although Cherie steadfastly remained in her casual clothes.

He was less circumspect when he went off to the annual News Corporation jamboree. He travelled to Hayman Island on the Great Barrier Reef to meet media mogul Rupert Murdoch and his satraps. The ostensible reason was to win over the New International titles – the *Sun*, the *Times*, the *Sunday Times* and the *News of the World* – and Sky Television to the New Labour cause. This he did, and it was much commented upon at the time. After all, there is nothing which so bedazzles the media as a story about the media.

What was not remarked upon was that for the bulk of the time there he was cruising amongst the glorious Whitsunday Islands. He was on a motor yacht which the then Australian Prime Minister, Paul Keating, had borrowed from one of his rich friends. I only knew because I had walked in on Anji Hunter and Kate Garvey as they sifted through the large number of photo snaps which their boss had brought back with him. Clearly, the island conference had been of great political importance. But I gained the impression that the sybaritic spell on the boat had made a deeper mark on Tony Blair.

Blair's tendency to gravitate towards the rich had struck me on two occasions, both of them involving members of the Moores family, beneficiaries of the Littlewoods pools and stores empire. On the occasion of a second visit to Liverpool Football Club, he asked me about David Moores, then chairman of the club. Blair questioned whether the chairman commanded much of a salary. I replied that I thought he was not paid anything at all. But, he continued, he cannot be very well off? I agreed that, according to an article in *Business Age* magazine, he was the poorest of the Moores family – he only had about £160 million. His eyes popped in his eagerness to know more about David.

On another occasion, David's more eccentric cousin, John, was invited to meet with the new leader. John was a long-standing Labour supporter and had been generous in his contributions to many Labour movement causes, including the party. I met John in the Central Lobby and took him to the leader's office, where we met Blair, along with his recently appointed chief of staff, Jonathan Powell. The leader's attempts at small talk fell flat as he struggled to make his usual impression on John. I needed to intervene repeatedly to keep any sort of conversation going.

Blair decided that he had something else scheduled and made off to his meeting, leaving us with Powell. To my astonishment Powell immediately and directly said to John: 'Right, how much will you give us?' I have never witnessed before or since a more gauche tap-up. John, naturally, was taken aback and managed to point out that he had always to the Labour Party, including £20,000 to the Labour Industry Forum, a fund run by Jack Cunningham and a former member of Parliament, Ken Weetch. Powell was obviously unaware of this and backed off. I was not surprised when, years later, I heard of the cash-for-peerages allegations.

Occasions like this should have woken me up to the type of politics I was associating with. Like many others, I failed to see the tawdry pattern which was emerging as the New Labour brand. Instinctively, I disliked many of the people who had become involved in the Blair project, yet I continued to make excuses for Blair himself, choosing to believe that if there were enough right-minded people nudging him, we could correct the political course he seemed to be taking into one that was more in line with traditional Labour values.

Even when he suddenly raised the totemic issue of Clause Four, I was one of many who was very relaxed about it. After all, I reasoned, nationalisation is a long-dead panacea. Issues like Network Rail and the banking crisis were to be in the future. Anyway, it seemed superfluous to have such a clause in the constitution when even theorists accepted the model of a mixed economy. Few of us looked for the thinking – of both Blair and Brown – which was behind the change and which was to create so many political problems in the years to come.

More than anything else, it was a conceit to believe that anyone could persuade Blair to change course once his mind was set on something. If Mrs Thatcher was not for turning, Tony Blair did not even give a backward glance. Naturally, he could not always get his own way, but in the early years as leader, he did seem to do so, primarily because no one wished to rock the boat as we headed towards inevitable victory. We won by-election after by-election as the Tories imploded. Our opinion poll ratings stayed at record highs, as those of the Major government slumped. It would have been a brave – or, rather, foolhardy – soul who queered the pitch with awkward questions – or gestures at that stage. Such was the determination to win that the Labour Party, both as individuals and collectively, disciplined itself in a way which was a gift to the New Labour revisionists – or, as they increasingly became known, the SDP Mark II.

Nevertheless, I would repeatedly try, when the opportunity occurred, to put a different view to Blair. Such an occasion arose when he decided to send his eldest son, Euan, to the Oratory School, a Catholic grant-maintained school. This had become a dividing line between the government and opposition. Labour party policy was to oppose grant-maintained status, yet here we had a leader defying that policy, saying that he was a father first and a party leader second.

Alastair Campbell had great difficulty with this. His wife was – and remains – a stalwart defender of the comprehensive ideal. Alastair agreed with her; but his boss went in the opposite direction and he had to defend him. He asked me to try to persuade Blair that he was making a mistake. I could speak as a parent, a Catholic, a school governor, schools spokesman and as a former teacher.

My 'persuasion' lasted all of thirty seconds. Blair just did not want to know and brushed me aside. Again, he had decided on a course of action and that was it. As far as he was concerned, it was not him that was out of step. It was for all of the rest of us to perform contortions on his contradictory practice, in his view. At least, nearly all of us. It was not the case for Harriet Harman who had sent one of her children to St Olave's in Kent – a grant-maintained selective school way out of her residential area. Little wonder that at one shadow Cabinet meeting, she had supported the return of the eleven-plus.

five

Don Dixon had told me of the two days of debate over the deputy chief whip's job. No one else ever mentioned to me that I was even considered for the job. Such is the way of such appointments, especially in government. Most of them are simply made and the appointees informed. How and why individuals are given such jobs rarely comes out. Mo Mowlam's appointment as shadow Secretary of State for Northern Ireland is a case in point.

I saw Mo walking towards the Members' Entrance after Blair had appointed his first team. 'What did you get?' I asked her.

'Northern Ireland,' she replied less than enthusiastically.

'Were you offered anything else?'

'No, nothing,' she shrugged and walked off. In my own mind,

I tried to rationalise it, recalling that Mo's doctorate had been on cantonisation in Switzerland.

Whether or not that was a factor in the view of Blair and his advisers, I would not have a clue. Presumably, some jobs were highly prized – shadow Chancellor, or shadow Foreign Secretary – whilst others were seen as a poisoned chalice. Rivalries at the top would need to be catered for, of course, keeping powerful but antagonistic personalities apart. There would be negotiations, or arguments, about filling shadow Cabinet posts.

Lower down, much depended upon patronage. Some shadow Cabinet members insisted on their own teams being composed of their friends and supporters; Brown and Prescott fell into this camp. Others took what was on offer. There was never a consistent or coherent pattern to these appointments. I certainly could not see it in my experience.

I was appointed schools spokesman under David Blunkett, who was shadow Education Secretary. Why this was I did not know, but I was happy to join a team of Blunkett, Bryan Davies and Estelle Morris. Bryan was a 'retread', an MP who had lost his seat, but who had fought to be re-elected. In between his elections, he had been full-time secretary to the Parliamentary Labour Party. Estelle was a former teacher, the daughter and niece of former MPs the Morris brothers.

Blunkett himself was a unique figure. Blind from birth, he had made his way through the Labour movement to make his mark on his home town of Sheffield. He became council leader during the turbulent 1980s, when he tried to arbitrate with the leadership of the Militant-controlled Liverpool City Council during its dispute with the government. I had met up with him in Salford to see how – if at all – we might achieve the seemingly impossible task of dissuading Liverpool City Council from its more extreme posturing. We were not to succeed at that time, but it was an early introduction which undoubtedly led to my joining the education team. Of course, I had other advantages. I had been a school teacher and a governor at St Francis Xavier's College, Liverpool, during a tense stand-off involving the NASUWT teaching union. I mistakenly thought I knew a little about education. Perhaps I did know a little about teaching, but knew barely anything about the politics of education.

Immersing myself in the subject, I was staggered by the vast number of interest groups, each with its own agenda and often at odds with other members of the huge education family. There were divisions between private and state schools, between religious schools and secular schools, between primary and secondary. Parents and governors had a view, as did headteachers. Various unions had views on just about everything, but rarely in agreement with each other. The Socialist Education Association would nationalise all private schools, whilst the latter wished to be unencumbered by the state in any shape or form whatsoever. It was a nightmare.

We would speak of schools as a collective, but they were no such thing. Each school was unique, with a head, staff and governors doing things in their own way, and that was just in the 27,000 schools then in the state system. The quality of education delivered was equally variable. There were excellent schools, adding value to each individual pupil, advancing academic excellence and promoting personal and emotional development.

Then there were the 'horror' schools, generally in the inner cities, or on sink estates, where the quality of education was abysmal. Alienated staff were just about controlling alienated youngsters, against a background of both aspirational and material poverty.

If parents were lucky, their children might just scramble onto the academic ladder. This was generally via a post code lottery, dependent upon where one lived. Overwhelmingly, the people who lost out most were the poor of the community.

My first job was to try to make sense of all this. Blunkett was busy from the start making contact with educational leaders – local education authorities, union bosses and academics. Besides, his disability did place some restrictions on his ability to assess the grass roots of educational provision. I decided to get out and about and visit schools and conferences throughout the country, and I did so for the next few years, from Northumberland in the north to Dorset on the south coast; from Lincolnshire and Kent in the east to Glamorgan in the west.

It was also a splendid basis on which to campaign – every constituency has schools in it. I took the opportunity to get to as many marginal constituencies as possible. I particularly targeted 'stand alone' seats. These were those which were way down our target list, and not considered close enough to merit regular visits from shadow Cabinet members. Yet these seats were vital to our impending success in 1997. A visit from an outside opposition politician drew the media, reassured the candidates and won over voters. It was an essential part of our campaigning strategy to get into as many 'stand alone' seats as often as we could.

One such seat was Selby in Yorkshire, where I saw the worst school building of all of those which I had seen. The Monk Fryston primary school was symbolic of the national crisis in our educational infrastructure. The school did a great job in a dire and dangerous building, ripe for demolition and replacement. Much to the consternation of the sitting Tory member of Parliament, who reported me to the Speaker, I visited the school with Labour candidate John Grogan. Happily the school is now replaced and Grogan is still the member for Selby.

Another seat which I visited was Scarborough & Whitby. I knew the sitting Conservative member, John Sykes, but was impressed by the energy of the Labour candidate, Laurie Quinn. The response he had from people in the street convinced me that he was campaigning very effectively. A fellow Scouser, Fiona Jones, was doing very well in Tory-held Newark and was to be rewarded with election success.

Not all, of course, were to meet the standards being demanded of candidates. When I visited the marginal of Peterborough, the candidate, Helen Brinton, did not turn up. There was little point in my pre-arranged school visit. The object was to promote the candidate, not me. I did note, however, that her campaigning team were from surrounding constituencies rather than Peterborough itself. There was clearly something amiss in the seat, so I was pleasantly surprised when we won it.

Nearer to home was the Bolton West constituency, a real Labour marginal. As well as my journeys around the country, I was asked by party HQ to keep an eye on some seats in the north-west, being a former regional organiser. Bolton West was one of them. They had chosen as candidate an unknown young woman named Ruth Kelly. On three different occasions, I went to the constituency for specific events. On each occasion, Kelly was missing. I told HQ that they could forget my mentoring such a candidate. Another member, Colin Pickthall, picked up that particular responsibility. I never dreamt that she would join the Cabinet. I am still baffled at how far she went on so little.

One front bench visit took me to Wisbech Grammar School, a beautiful school in a beautiful setting. I travelled on to two seats on the Norfolk coast, Great Yarmouth and Waveney. The tyranny of distance – even in England – was brought home to me travelling that long, single-lane road from Downham Market to Great Yarmouth. My journey ended in a traditional Labour way, with a makeshift bed in a party member's front room! Yet the candidates were keen, well briefed and well organised. Needless to say they both won their seats from the Conservative incumbents.

It was very debilitating to drive so many miles, but it was the only practical way of covering the country. I would often be asked on my visits about my driver. Equally often, my questioner would be greatly surprised when I said that I drove myself everywhere! Many of my visits were to seats held by Conservatives. Individuals like Bob Dunn and Jacques Arnold joined Michael Alison in condemning me to the Speaker for breaking parliamentary protocol, but I never did. I was simply campaigning for my party. I loved it, as I enjoyed visiting a fabulous cross-section of England and Wales.

However, I cannot say that I always enjoyed visiting the various education conferences, a 'must' in a politician's diary. The National Union of Teachers conference was a real bore. It seemed to be dominated by Trotskyite teachers from inner London, who were intent on howling down anyone who took issue with their views. On one occasion, I saw an opportunity to use this fringe to maximise political support for our education policies.

The conference in question was in Blackpool at the Winter Gardens. I knew it well from my time as north-west regional organiser, responsible for security at the Labour Party annual conference at the venue. On the occasion in question, I had arrived before Blunkett to find his adviser, Conor Ryan, panicking about a hostile 'welcoming' crowd awaiting Blunkett's arrival. It had been arranged for Blunkett to arrive via a side entrance, but I insisted he came through the front. I then told the teachers that, despite their disbelief, he would be coming in through the main entrance. I also tipped off the press.

When Blunkett arrived, he was met by a very noisy crowd of protestors. We guided him in, and into a side office, with the protestors kept out. It was noisy but not in any way dangerous. The papers, however, painted a very different picture. This 'blind man' had been jostled and threatened by an angry crowd. Not really, but all of the sympathy was with him and public curiosity was directed towards the union activists who had picketed the entrance, and the union leadership, which seemed unable to control their members.

I would not like to give the impression that the media were always so friendly towards the Labour education team. I attended one NASUWT conference in Torquay. The night before my speech, I was besieged by a group of journalists, led by David Wooding of the *Sun*, determined to get a story on grant-maintained schools. They were hoping for a faux pas from me and, in order to do so, plied me with alcoholic drinks. Naturally, I took the drinks offered, but gave them no return in the form of a useable quote. It was very gratifying to see the same journalists in the press box looking very hungover the following morning as I delivered my speech.

It was not all gallivanting around the country. We had our parliamentary commitments to keep, including Education Questions, when we would attempt to put killer questions to education ministers, led by Gillian Shephard, her team including Eric Forth, Robin Squire and Cheryl Gillan. They were actually a likeable group of people. Gillian herself was enormously amiable, perhaps too much so for a front-rank secretary of state. Eric was tough but fair, capable of operating without a brief. A staunch fan of Elvis Presley, he would proudly highlight his own upbringing in a Glasgow tenement to any class warriors on our side. Robin would agonise about being fair, and was as likeable as his boss. His wife was a Labour supporter and he was very much on the left of the then Conservative Party. Cheryl was the junior in the group. I was able on one occasion to get a Cup Final ticket for her husband, a Manchester United fan. Such are the peculiarities of parliamentary life.

Our own team became augmented when employment was fused with education. In came Stephen Byers and Ian McCartney. We would have team meetings on a weekly basis, although I confess to not having read enough into what was being said at them. I was, perhaps, too content with the roving role of ambassador for the education team. I thought little of the politics that were happening around me.

Others attended these meetings. One was Margaret Hodge, who had no official role but who had persuaded Blunkett that she had something to offer. She would often be accompanied by her young researcher, Stephen Twigg, later to defeat Portillo in 1997.

Another, more ominous, attendee was Conor Ryan, Blunkett's adviser. He was a man with whom I found it difficult to relate. I was later to discover just how involved he was with the whole New Labour project. It appeared that Blunkett relied quite heavily on his advice and on that of Sophie Linden, another of his researchers/advisers. I understood his dependency. No matter what he or anyone else says, it must be incredibly difficult to be blind and to act independently. All decent politicians take advice; I just believe that he needed more.

Ryan spent a great deal of time talking with Stephen Byers and Estelle Morris, but very little with me. There were a number of reasons. Firstly, he had written me off from the start. Perhaps he thought I was not up to the job. Secondly, my politics would never mesh with those of New Labour, and there was little to discuss, especially given my trenchant criticism of New Labour and its adherents. Perhaps he just did not like me – he was an Irish snob, and the Liverpool Irish would be anathema to him.

All of this is speculation long after the fact. The truth is that I was happy slogging around the country, and had little time for the nuanced machinations of Westminster. What I could not help but notice was the distance growing between Blunkett and me. There was never a showdown – it just became a more formal relationship over time. During my early days in his team, his son, Alistair, had completed a foundation course at Liverpool University. Whilst he did so, he stayed in my family home. On one occasion, he and his father took my family into Liverpool city centre for a birthday meal, whilst I was whipped for a vote in Parliament. Nevertheless, such familiarity can easily turn sour, especially in Westminster.

At this time, I also had responsibility for youth policy and sketched an outline of what I thought might be the basis of our approach. Unfortunately, it clashed with a policy written on the back of a fag packet at an IPPR function attended by the shadow Chancellor, and unknown to me. Such was the birth of the New Deal policy, which purported to give work, education or training to all of our young people. As was his habit, Brown announced this without talking to anyone, or working the ideas through.

Mo Mowlam and I both had a locus in this – she was chair of the National Executive's Youth Committee and I, ostensibly, was responsible for youth policy. We decided to write to him jointly, expressing our concerns. Weeks went by and we had no reply. I wrote again, along with a copy of the original letter and circulars emanating from his office on the subject of the New Deal. Again, there was no response.

I needed to go to the leader's office on a different matter. Brown was leaving as I arrived. Looking embarrassed, he mumbled that he had received my letter and enclosures, but said they were not from him. I was astounded. 'How can they not be from you, when they have Ed Balls's and Ed Miliband's names on them, with your office number on them too, and they are on your headed notepaper?' I queried.

'I never signed them,' he said as he turned and walked away. I simply concluded that the man was in denial, by choice.

The leader, on the other hand, took more of an interest in education than a shadow Chancellor in denial. Indeed, Blair's liking for soundbites gave him his political priority of 'education, education, education'. This was not lost on his education team, who reacted, intriguingly, in different ways. Blunkett became almost sycophantic about whatever superficiality Blair uttered. Byers, on the other hand, took more and more interest in education, although his brief was employment.

Increasingly, the team meetings were less relaxed than they had been. There was more testing of positions far outside the education or employment briefs. Views on Europe or the wider economy were sought by Blunkett. It was as if we were being examined as to our suitability for more than education. It was quite perplexing at the time for the more simple minded members of our little confraternity.

One of the less attractive developments of that period was increasing acrimony between David Blunkett and Roy Hattersley. This revolved around educational policy concerning comprehensive schools. Hattersley felt that we were selling out on the principle. Blunkett had said: 'Read my lips; no more selection.' This statement had been popularly understood to mean that selection was to be phased out completely. Blunkett's redefinition was that he meant that no more schools, other than those already selecting, would be allowed to select.

It came to a crunch at Conference, when I felt duty bound to defend Blunkett, although reluctantly, after Hattersley had attacked him on the issue. In my heart of hearts, I knew then that I was on the wrong side of the policy divide on this issue. Nevertheless, I did feel strongly that a split in the education team at the annual conference was mightily dangerous, given that about one in three of our members at that time had a direct connection to education. I bit my tongue and stuck up for Blunkett.

One of the more difficult parts of my brief was dealing with the private sector. I had attended a fee-paying school – a direct grant school, run by the Christian Brothers. I had arrived there by virtue of the eleven-plus, another great evil in the Labour Party catechism. I had also taught in private schools in Australia, but nothing had prepared me for the private sector in England and Wales.

There were so many elements to it: the specialist schools for the disabled, or religious schools, or just those with singular educational philosophies. We tend to think of the great public schools and their imitators, when these are but a section of the private education sector. Nevertheless, as with state schools, I tried to visit as many as I could, as well as the organisations which try to represent their interests.

Some were hostile, like the organisation of grant-maintained schools headed by Brother Francis, former principal of St Francis Xavier's College, Liverpool, where I had been a governor. This school was the first to 'opt out' of the local council under grant-maintained legislation. I had led the opposition to the first ballot, which we, the opponents, won. However, a second ballot went the other way, hardly surprising given the many advantages afforded to supporters of 'opt outs' in the ballot provisions of the government's legislation on grant-maintained schools.

Others were more open, understandably waiting to maintain their position and fearful of what a Labour government might mean for them. Our undertaking was clear on assisted places, for example. No one on assisted places finance would have that finance removed before they had completed their education. I gave that assurance repeatedly and wrote to the private schools to that effect. Little did I know that my words were to be quoted like a latter-day Zinoviev letter when we came into government.

One part of our responsibilities was to oppose government legislation where it was incompatible with Labour Party policy. The Grant Maintained Schools and Nursery Education Bill certainly fell into that category – or, at least, the part of it seeking to extend grant-maintained schools did. It was my job to lead the opposition in committee, ably supported by Estelle Morris and a team of backbenchers. Leading for the government was Eric Forth, assisted by Robin Squire and Cheryl Gillan.

Eric was a fierce opponent, but always fair. He was a politician to his finger nails, leaving the purely educational arguments to Robin, with Cheryl picking up any pieces which fell through the net. Their whip on the committee was a West Midlands member, Anthony Coombes. Unfortunately for the government, he was a very poor whip. We beat the government in the final stages of the Bill in committee. The whip had gone in search of a missing Tory committee member. The Tory chairman of the committee lost his patience with the missing members, and ordered the doors locked and the vote to be taken. As a result, we won the vote, cancelling out huge chunks of the Bill.

Forth was relaxed, intending to restore the Bill in its entirety at report stage on the floor of the House of Commons. I checked with

Dewar, our chief whip. Did we have the numbers for an early vote? He doubted it and was unenthusiastic about an early vote. However, I had heard from Tory sources that they were not expecting a vote until later in the evening – they expected a protracted debate on the contentious legislation.

An old mining member, Geoffrey Lofthouse, was in the chair for the report stage, as a deputy Speaker. I simply stood and said that we had already exercised the arguments ad nauseam in committee, and therefore 'moved the vote', an old trade union expression straight out of Citrine with which Geoff was familiar but the Tories obviously were not. They simply sat in their places, stunned. If they possessed had their usual presence of mind, Eric Forth et al. would have been up on their feet on some pretext to keep things going until they could get their act together. They did not, and the deputy Speaker called 'Division'.

Again, Dewar voiced his scepticism, but when the tellers reported the result, Labour had won by one vote. Even then, there was a sting in the tale. The Tory teller, the hapless Anthony Coombes, had miscounted by one. If he had counted correctly, the Speaker's casting vote would have gone by convention to the government, saving their legislation. Such is the House of Commons.

I was overjoyed, but irritated by a clearly confused Mandelson asking of no one in particular: 'But I thought we were supportive of this Bill?' It depends on who 'we' were. I always believe that, like their entryist predecessors, New Labour cultists had a separate agenda from that of the official party policy. It was never definitive – to write it down would be too constrictive – and would be at odds with the infinitely flexible 'principles' of the New Labour architects.

Right up to election day – and beyond – I dutifully attended the round of education conferences, where I had become well known and well received. I had two conferences left in my diary: the National Association of Schoolmasters and, on the day after the election, the Parent Teacher Confederation conference, scheduled for Liverpool. I was disturbed, however, to hear that Byers was penned in to cover press and television one weekend, billed as the shadow schools minister.

I tried without success to reach Blunkett to have this out. Instead, Ryan, his *eminence grise*, came on to me in a weak effort to explain this 'misunderstanding'. I sent him packing and told him to have his boss send Byers to my outstanding education commitments. I realised, of course, that I was out and Byers was into my shoes. Why that was I was never to know. What riled me was that Blunkett never had the guts to tell me that, after three years of hard and loyal graft, I was to be out of his team.

Despite my disgust, I relented. For the sake of the election campaign we were fighting, I resolved to stay quiet and meet my diary commitments. At the Liverpool conference, the election result showed a landslide Labour win. Delegates asked about my new job. I told them in truth that I expected nothing. No one was guaranteed a ministerial post. If I was to be offered anything, I thought, I knew it would not be in education.

six

May 2 1997. Another bright sunny day, celebrating an astounding Labour landslide. Naturally, all of the attention was on the Blair family's entry into Downing Street, symbolising the end of eighteen years of Tory hegemony. Carefully choreographed with a 'crowd' of Labour Party workers and supporters in attendance, the triumphal passage of the Blairs into the prime ministerial residence made great television, and appeared – as it was intended – to represent a whole new approach to politics.

I had spent the previous night firstly at my own constituency count and thereafter with my party workers at the Mere Lane Social Club. There were numerous radios at the count, with everyone anxious to keep up with developments elsewhere. The first result in was Chris Mullin's seat in Sunderland. It showed a sharply increased majority, and that set a remarkable trend. Shortly afterwards, the Merseyside seat of Crosby, a 'stand alone' seat, was declared as a Labour gain. I could hardly believe it, given its reputation as solidly anti-Labour and with a popular Conservative member in Sir Malcolm Thornton. I knew we were onto something big.

My own result gave me over 78 per cent of the vote and a 29,000 majority. What counted, however, were the marginal seats which just kept falling to Labour. I went on to the Mere Lane club to follow the television coverage. Seats I had visited in Brighton, Medway, Norfolk, Nottingham, Yorkshire, the East and West Midlands – unbelievably, they were all turning to Labour. The television showed the bitterness of our opponents, personified in the abuse thrown between Jimmy Goldsmith and David Mellor. Then came the shock of shocks – Margaret Hodge's researcher, Stephen Twigg, had dethroned Michael Portillo! It was a massacre of the Tories.

So it was that our hopes were raised to impossible heights. I had my own political gripes, but this was a time for optimism, not carping by individuals. With all of my personal doubts, I still did my conference duty the following morning. As a sensible precaution, I kept my mobile telephone on and with me, just in case No. 10 calls, as I joked with the conference; but no call came at any time on that Friday.

On the Saturday, I tried to have a 'normal' day, probably the first after virtually three years' solid campaigning. I did very little other than a bit of gardening. Still the phone did not ring, until late in the day, when Blunkett , of all people, called. He asked me if I had heard from Downing Street. I told him that I had not. He then expressed surprise and told me he understood that I was going into Defence. He rang off, saying he would find out what was happening.

I had never even wondered about Defence; it was not on my wish list and I had expressed no interest in that subject area during my time in Parliament. Still, I thought, I can only wait and see. Late on Sunday morning I had another call, from the No. 10 switchboard, asking me to stand by. After a while the operator came back on and told me the call had been halted. Later in the day, the switchboard again contacted me, asking me to stand by for a call – they would ring me back. Again, nothing came of it and I was about to give up any hope of a government job.

Then on the Monday morning, Blair phoned, offering me a job in the Cabinet Office. I was in no position to bargain and I immediately said yes.

Although I unhesitatingly accepted, I knew nothing of the work of the Cabinet Office, or of the ministers within it. I soon discovered that I would be working with David Clarke, who had been made Chancellor of the Duchy of Lancaster, and that the dread Mandelson would be based in the Cabinet Office as Minister without Portfolio. I would be the parliamentary secretary to the Cabinet Office. I arranged to go the very next day.

Arriving at the door of the Cabinet Office on Whitehall, I was met by a suave and smiling young man, Justin McLaren. He was, I discovered, my private secretary, although when he addressed me as 'Minister', I instinctively glanced over my shoulder for the object of his appellation. I still could not quite take in my new designation.

My office was palatial. After my years on the roof of the Commons, this was luxury indeed. Justin reappeared with the assistant private secretary, and they both started to question me. Here we go, I thought. There will be a raft of searching queries before I am let loose on departmental business. I was quite wrong. As the two civil servants noted down my answers intently, I was asked if I preferred tea or coffee, with or without milk and sugar, and my favourite alcoholic tipple.

Justin turned out to be quite a character. His former girlfriend was another civil servant named Ffion, who had dumped him for a rising Tory star, William Hague. Eventually he became press officer to Stephen Norris when he stood for Mayor of London. Although a Conservative, he was an extremely loyal and industrious private secretary to me. A provincial like myself, his goal in coming to London had not been to be a civil servant, but to be a rock guitarist. Like his eventual successors as my private secretary, he was a multi-talented individual. His immediate successor was a saxophonist in a big band, and he was followed by a part-time scuba diving instructor! These young fast-track civil servants gave me a wholly new perspective on Whitehall and its possibilities.

However, the question immediately arose: what was I to do in this new job? There was not a sheet of paper on policy to be had; nor was it as if there was a job description available. Fortunately, the senior civil servants in the department were trawling through our election manifesto to see what tasks were appropriate to the Cabinet Office. They were well practised at reading such runes. Besides, there was the ongoing departmental work to be maintained. That did not simply stop because of a change of government. It meant that there were departments and agencies to visit, and people to be met.

Initially it was difficult because it appeared that David Clarke wanted to do virtually everything in the department. Mandelson was quite separate from us, although housed in our department. I felt quite dispirited with little to do, and explained my frustration to my permanent secretary, Robin Mountfield. A native of Merseyside himself, he understood, and quickly the balance of responsibilities altered. I took on virtually all of the agencies run through the Cabinet Office, and they kept me very busy.

It remained an odd situation in that office. There was a

semi-detached Mandelson, an increasingly anxious Clarke and myself. Clarke believed from the start that Mandelson was undermining him; and he *was* being undermined. His first weekend in post was marred by stories in the press saying that he was not to be in government for long. Along with others, including Ann Taylor and Jack Cunningham, he was said to be in government under sufferance, gaining his post only because of the convention whereby the first Cabinet consists of members of the former parliamentary committee. His anxiety revealed itself in verbal fights with senior civil servants and, on one occasion, he got his special adviser to search through waste bins for 'evidence' of plots by civil servants against him.

As a Cabinet member, one would have expected him to have regular liaison with the Prime Minister. In fact, he told me that he had never had a one-to-one with Blair. This was embarrassing to me personally, as I had taken several meetings with Blair in the course of my duties. After all, there was only a door between the Cabinet Office and Number 10. Mandelson was in Downing Street every day for some reason or another; yet the Cabinet member in our department was sidelined by the Prime Minister.

Other former members of the parliamentary committee were also ignored, without even nominal membership of the Cabinet. Blair was never enamoured of either Gavin Strang or Michael Meacher. As a result, both were denied departments of their own to run, despite convention. These were signposts that Blair was determined to shape his own government.

Within days of our accession to government, I had an unannounced visit from the Cabinet secretary, Robin Butler. Nearing the end of his time in office, he still took a great interest in the new government. I assumed that he had dropped by in order to weigh me up. What he decided over a cup of tea I will never know, but thereafter he was always a most agreeable man to meet with.

*   *   *

The work began to fall into place. I needed to do some things which I had never anticipated, like closing down an agency. In fact, I was the first minister to actually shut down civil service jobs in that government. The agency in question was a security agency known by the acronym SAFE. It had itself been composed of jobs which did not fit neatly into any other of the myriad agencies which operate under the aegis of Whitehall. I recognised that it was superfluous and closed it, but with two conditions. There was to be full protection of the workforce under TUPE rules and there were to be no compulsory redundancies. I called the workforce together, told them of my decision and answered questions. They took a difficult decision extremely well. I think that they were glad to end the uncertainty which had bedevilled them for some years.

At this time, I also made my first foreign trip as a Minister. One of my agencies was the Civil Service College, which, in partnership with the new Department for International Development, was doing great things in improving governance overseas. I was also responsible for ICT in government at that time. Accordingly, I went off to Malaysia and Singapore to see both sides of this brief in action.

Early one morning of departure, my flat telephone rang. It was Justin, to tell me what had happened to Princess Diana. He had also checked with No. 10 to see if I should cancel my trip. They said it should go ahead, so off I went to Heathrow, where I was taken, as a minister, to the VIP lounge. There was only one other person there.

It was Margaret Thatcher. Fiddling with the television set, she did not even look up, but said to me: 'Where are you going to?'

I replied: 'Malaysia.'

'Have you checked with No. 10?'

Not that it was any of her business, but I answered: 'Yes – they have told me to go.'

'Oh, good. I'm off to America myself. Goodbye.' With that she left me alone with my thoughts.

The trip itself was largely uneventful, although it was my first experience of staying in an embassy or high commission. I thought that the standard was extraordinarily high for guest accommodation. The experience was to repeat itself wherever I went. Perhaps my expectations were just too low, but I was taken by the level of comfort afforded to ministers when abroad.

Another exotic trip on government business took me to South Africa – the first Labour minister to visit since Denis Healey had been there twenty years before. Technically, I was not the first minister to visit, but first to visit officially. Clare Short had been on a private visit earlier, to see her sister, I was told; but it was very low key with no official recognition of her presence at all. She would not have it.

I had the honour of sitting in Mandela's box in Parliament as a visitor. In the box alongside was the famous American singing group the Temptations. It was flattering when the Speaker called Parliament's attention to my presence and to that of the Temptations. I became alarmed when a PNC member moved that we not be allowed to leave until we sang a song. This was obviously aimed at the Temptations and not meant to be taken seriously!

This was at the time of Bill Clinton's visit to South Africa. I happened to talk to one of his security chiefs in Cape Town. The

Americans had booked out four harbour-side hotels and had an equal number of helicopters to ferry Clinton and Mandela out to Robben Island. 'Why the overkill?' I asked the chief.

'To confuse any would-be assassins,' he answered. When I said that I believed it was Americans who killed American presidents, he turned on his heels, unamused, and left me.

One other trip worthy of note was a visit to Seattle as a guest of Microsoft. The company aggressively markets its products, and its ambition was to have a major country using only its products as a platform for all of its information technology needs. It had American states and cities, as well as many international examples of its products' usefulness. However, a national government was a prize to behold.

Its new chief operations officer was a cross between a chat show host and a stand-up comic. He had previously worked for Procter and Gamble, selling washing power. In the middle of an anti-trust action, Microsoft had realised that change was required. The man at the top, however, remained Bill Gates, and I was invited to meet him. He kept the top floors of Westin Towers as his Seattle place, and his security was high. Nevertheless, it is not every day that one gets a meeting with the richest man in the world. He was, however, a little disappointing. Mix the Mekon in with Alfred E. Neuman and you get the picture – a very astute, but nerdish, character who speaks a lot like a small-town technophile. I left him saying: 'Hey, Pete. That was neat – we gotta do it again.' No thanks, I thought.

Meanwhile, change did come to the Cabinet Office. David Clarke's long predicted demise happened, but later than anticipated. A reshuffle was scheduled for before the summer recess, and the Prime Minister had pencilled in a Downing Street reception for his new formation. Unfortunately for him, difficulties with senior members of his team meant that the reshuffle was delayed. David Clarke was at the reception with his wife, who was angry at the way in which her husband had been treated.

The reception was held in No. 10. Blair appeared, stood on a box and gave a short speech of no great consequence. As he finished, the chatter resumed. My wife and I were talking to Kate Garvey when an anxious Prime Minister appeared at our side. He was enquiring after his wife's whereabouts. Kate said that she thought she was upstairs in the family flat. As Blair dashed off in pursuit of his missing wife, she appeared calm and chatty from another doorway. I presumed that they had had a difference of opinion which bothered him far more than it did her.

When the reshuffle did come, Jack Cunningham replaced Clarke. Jack really was a one-off. As soon as he arrived, he decided that his office was not grand enough and ordered a complete change in who went where. The large central office, which had previously housed both his private office and mine, was to be refurbished for his sole use. A private bathroom was to be added, and I was to move to the floor below. The net result was a grand office for a grand man.

On his first day in the department, I undertook to show Jack around and to brief him. I could not help but notice a huge bouquet of flowers which had arrived in the name of the Hinduja brothers. I told Jack of the presence of the 'spooks' on the fourth floor and of the story of Heseltine's office. The latter was a large conference room now, but was allegedly the only room in the building which was not – or could not be – bugged. Hence, Heseltine had made it his office.

I went on to tell Jack that it was said that all telephones in the building were bugged. Jack's retort was a succinct 'Bollocks!' Like all ministers, he understood that his calls would be monitored by his private office; but he could not accept that there was anyone else listening in.

Some weeks later, he told me that he had found a second wire running down from his desk telephone to the floor and under the carpet. He lifted the carpet – an image highly amusing in itself – to find that the cable went under the floorboards. He apparently took up a board to see the wire go into a box marked MOD. He asked the staff about this, only to be told that 'MOD' signified the manufacturer of the kit and that there was nothing to be concerned about.

Cunningham was not a diligent worker like David Clarke. To use his own words, he was a 'big picture man', irritated by detail, which he preferred to leave to menials like me. For example, he inherited the 'Modernising Government' agenda, but took little interest in it. When we met various Cabinet members to brief them on it, he would make some remarks – sweeping generalisations – and then hand on to me for the detail. When we met with Mo Mowlam, she was openly insulting to him, asking me in colourful language how I put up with him. That was Mo.

We also had a new permanent secretary in Brian Bender, who also originated in Liverpool. Like the retired Robin Mountfield, he was a consummate permanent secretary, moving effortlessly from subject to subject, and department to department, with barely a discernible ripple. I imagine that it would be very difficult for officials to deal with a headstrong minister. Not that only ministers were headstrong. I had certainly witnessed senior civil servants losing their tempers in debates with ministers. Yet it was dangerous for either minister or civil servant to do so. They had a symbiotic relationship.

What I never understood, and indeed disliked, was the seamless transition from senior civil servant to consultant, or private sector employee. Take Lucy Neville-Rolfe, for instance. She was a senior civil servant when Labour came into office, responsible for working up the practicalities of a Foods Standards Agency. She married the permanent secretary at the then Ministry for Agriculture, Fisheries and Food. She told us one day that she was leaving the Cabinet Office to take up a post as director of government relations at Tesco. This was not untypical – after all, her acknowledged expertise would have been in great demand in the private sector. Yet I would have thought that there was a clear conflict of interest involved. I know that ministers have always taken up posts associated with their briefs, but only after a healthy time lapse following the end of their ministerial career.

This culture bothered me because of the narrowing of the role of senior civil servants. They no longer ran things – such enterprises as they did run had either been privatised, or hived off into an agency. Ultimately, their role was to advise ministers. The latter already had advisers – so-called special advisers, the number and role of whom had rapidly expanded. Civil service advice seemed too often to pass the buck, by either calling in consultants or setting up another quango. On rare occasions, a 'czar' was appointed in a given area. One such was Peter Gershon.

He had been chief operating officer at Marconi, a company which had spectacularly failed. Although a pleasant enough man in himself, I could not but think it was an odd background for a man who was to recommend a new structure for government procurement of goods and services. Yet that was precisely his remit. The result was the Office of Government Commerce, and its first director was. . . Peter Gershon.

We dealt with a lot of government appointments in the Cabinet Office. It was my job to deputise for the Prime Minister in dealing with the civil service, and what he wanted he generally got. For example, the commissioner for appointments when we came into government was Sir Fred Peach. He was the man who told me that a trade union leader would not have the appropriate experience to chair a quango! When his successor was sought, the Prime Minister wanted Dame Rennie Fritchie to succeed him. Despite my profound doubts, he had his way and, technically at least, I appointed her.

Blair did not always see it as him having his way. Indeed, at one meeting with him, Jonathan Powell, new Cabinet secretary Sir Richard Wilson and Jack Cunningham, I heard him echo Mrs Thatcher, complaining that he could get nothing done. He was not the first – nor would he be the last – Prime Minister to be frustrated by the civil service. Sir Richard Wilson struck me as being very adept at the black arts of Sir Humphrey.

This was a man who bought himself (on the taxpayer, of course) a hackney cab, so that he might more easily work on his way to and from the office. This novelty did not last long before the cab was parked up for some weeks in the Cabinet Office, before being sold off. This was also the non-political civil servant who tipped me the wink about a deal done between Brown and Byers, in the hope that I would tip off a bypassed Prescott (away snorkelling in the Maldives). As it happened, I had no need. Dick Caborn told me in the House of Commons cloakroom that Prescott had already discovered the treacherous deal and had communicated his ire directly to Brown.

In those days, he was not the only senior minister to lose his patience with the Chancellor. At Brown's first Christmas party, a miffed Blunkett turned up demanding of all and sundry the opportunity to punch Brown on the nose. Brown diplomatically disappeared until his angry 'guest' had departed.

In those early days, Brown was constantly holding receptions, inviting rank and file party members from around the country. It was as if he was running a delayed leadership campaign. I told Blair of this 'campaign' and of its destabilising effect. It did not seem to sink in at the time, but he eventually understood that he needed to constantly woo his own supporters. I suggested he meet his backbenchers in groups of twenty or so.

He took this up, and the first group happily came to Downing Street to express their views to their leader. However, rather than simply listen, Blair seemed to want to argue the toss with each of them. Subsequently, he asked me how I thought it had gone. Disastrously, I said. I pointed out that I had walked back to the House with half a dozen of them. Anticipating reassurance on the way to Downing Street, they left in a somewhat confused state.

He had a similar effect on junior ministers. I suggested that he meet with them. They were very often isolated within their departments, I argued, and would benefit from a direct line to the Prime Minister. Again, it was as if Blair wanted to argue with his own ministers. To make matters worse, Jack Cunningham who chaired the meeting, went on and on, using up the valuable time available for the junior ministers. Only Charlie Falconer, who had taken over Mandelson's role, had any sense that a golden opportunity was being missed.

What was clear to me was that Blair was still uncomfortable with larger groups of his own troops. He was also ill at ease with any criticism, no matter how constructive or well-meaning. I had the impression that he thought that members and ministers should simply fall in behind anything he proposed or wanted. Where there was any sort of difficulty, it was for others to make accommodations, not him.

One exception to this was the first Christmas in No. 10. I suggested a Christmas party for disabled children in care. The Blairs liked the idea, but the staff in No. 10 did not. They threw up every possible obstacle and even insisted on using their own costly caterers, even though I had obtained a reputable caterer for free. Hamleys were already on board, donating free gifts for each child. It took the personal intervention of the Prime Minister for the event to take place – and I was to be Father Christmas.

It was an excellent party. Both of the Blairs attended and played their full part. I made a suitably portly Father Christmas, complete with my voluminous white whiskers. Upon leaving the party, I slipped through the door between No. 10 and the Cabinet Office. Facing that door was the office of the Cabinet secretary, where he was hosting his own Christmas party. Spotting me, or rather, me as Father Christmas, he invited me to join him for a drink which I did. Strangely, no one questioned the presence of a minister dressed as Father Christmas. Their easy formality was a wonder to behold.

However, all good things come to an end, and my time in the Cabinet Office was indeed good. Firstly, it was, by and large, staffed by outstanding people – friendly, bright and co-operative. Secondly, it was a marvellous vantage point from which to learn and to observe what was happening right across government. After all, between the three of us in the department we sat on all Cabinet committees and shared their papers. Finally, it was a very varied department. Whether dealing with ministerial cars, foreign governments or the buildings in Whitehall, we seemed to have our fingers in every pie. I was sorry to leave.

When I did leave, I discovered my fate from Jack Cunningham. He had genuinely believed that he was being dropped in the reshuffle of 1999. When the Prime Minister rang, he was very relieved to be told that he was staying, but that I was going. He did not know where but my answer came that evening.

seven

I could not be sure that I was going anywhere in government that evening. In frustration, I rang Charlie Falconer to voice my discontent at not knowing. When the call did come, I was offered a job in Defence. My instinct was to say no, but a quick reality check told me I had nothing to bargain with. It seemed at best a sideways move, although in personal terms, it was a backward step. I again rang Charlie and shared my thoughts before setting off home. I was leaving for my annual family holiday the next day.

As I drove to the ferry port at Dover the following morning, my mobile went. I pulled over and took the call. It was Anji Hunter. Charlie had obviously told her that I was miffed. She asked how I felt, and I told her in all honesty that I did not fancy Defence. She was very positive, telling me how well I would get on with George

Robertson and John Spellar. Little did she know of my disputes with both of them. Besides, the only job left was in Northern Ireland. With a family to consider, that was even less attractive than Defence. I resigned myself to Defence, but asked who they had in mind for Northern Ireland if not me. The reply was that no one was yet earmarked for it. I suggested George Howarth, who had told me despondently earlier that morning that he had lost his Home Office post. He got the job.

Northern Ireland had been the bailiwick of Mo Mowlam, and she had proved enormously popular and successful. She remained true to her mischievous self whilst there. Her four bodyguards she referred to as 'Shirley, Shirley, Shirley and Shirley'. They just smiled – she won people over. I had spent a weekend at Hillsborough Castle as her guest, along with my wife and youngest son. It was an eclectic house party: Jeremy Irons and his wife, Sinéad Cusack, Richard Coles of the Communards (now a vicar!), Mo's brain surgeon, Mark Glaser, Larry Whitty and his wife, a friend from a local pub in Mo's Redcar constituency, and three MPs – Joyce Quinn, Janet Anderson and her partner, Jim Dowd – together with Mo's husband, Jon Norton.

I distinguished myself by sinking *Tom King* – not the Tory grandee, but the boat named after him and used on the lake at Hillsborough. I had decided to take my son for a leisurely row around the lake. Unfortunately, I tripped as I got into the boat, turning it over and dumping my son and I into the lake! I heaved him out onto dry land, and then myself. Returning to the castle to dry out, it was my luck that a *Times* reporter should call in on some matter. However, reportage of my aquatic endeavours painted me as a child-rescuing hero rather than a clumsy fool who nearly drowned himself and his son. Such are the wonders of spin!

Needless to say, I needed to speak with my new boss, George

Robertson, and I did so using my mobile from a cross-channel ferry. Our conversation consisted of the usual pleasantries, with him wishing me a refreshing holiday and looking forward to the new team 'taking forward' the Strategic Defence Review. I was not overjoyed at the prospect, but that was the roll of the political dice. In fact, I spent much of my holiday reflecting on my time in the Cabinet Office rather than my future in the Ministry of Defence. My two eventful years had been enjoyable and, in some ways, remarkable.

I knew that ministers were time limited in any one job. It is one of the more remarkable facets of the British system of government that ministers carry responsibility but relatively little power. Rarely does a minister see her or his own initiative through to fruition; but that same minister takes the rap for the failings of his or her predecessor. Most tellingly, the secretary of state may be theoretically head of a department of state, but the permanent secretary is the accounting officer; and that gives the latter enormous power.

I experienced this over a surplus hospital in Bristol. A group of local charities wanted to buy the building for work with the disabled. They had agreed a price with the agency responsible, which was under my charge. However, the agency had raised the price, seemingly arbitrarily. Local MPs approached me on the issue. I called in the head of the agency for an explanation. He said the market price had risen and he was loyally bound to get the best price for the property. A new price was agreed, but again the price rose. A second time, the charities made up the new demand, only to be gazumped yet again.

I took this up with officials and the permanent secretary. I wanted to fix a price, but they would have none of it. If I were to try to do so, the permanent secretary would be obliged to write to the National Audit Office, who in turn would put in a report to the Public Accounts Committee. Ultimately, I would be personally responsible for any notional loss due to my intemperate decision – 'a promising career derailed' as it was put to me.

I felt quite chastened. Later that day, I happened by chance to see Bob Sheldon, a distinguished former chairman of the PAC and now in the Lords. I explained my position to him, and he confirmed exactly what I had been told by my permanent secretary. As I turned to walk away, he told me that there was another way, to my surprise. He advised me, on my return to the department, to speak with the permanent secretary, saying that I had spoken to Bob and that his advice was in line with that of the department, but then to tell him that, rather than sell the property, we would in effect give it away – at least in part.

His advice worked like a dream. The permanent secretary was well pleased that Bob Sheldon had confirmed his advice. Then came the bombshell: 'but Bob advised me that I could give away the difference between the price originally agreed and the price asked by the agency'. There was barely a flicker from the permanent secretary – a Sir Humphrey pause – and then the assurance that the papers would be drawn up right away. As simple as that.

The mechanism was straightforward. An order would be drawn up giving effect to that decision. It would then join a host of other orders going for the approval of the House of Commons at the end of play on a Friday. It would be rare for there to be more than three or four members present then, and there could be very many orders. Only if a member present objected would that order be halted, and that was extremely unlikely. The net effect would be that I had not made such a decision, but the House of Commons had.

This was a classic example of the power of those who know how to use the system to the best effect. Bob Sheldon was a rarity in his intimate knowledge of such matters. Most members have not a clue as to how the House operates, certainly in that kind of detail. Naturally, the mandarins were aware of how to get things through Parliament when they needed to, as they knew how to push things through government. Presumably, that is why the Cabinet secretary convenes his own meeting of permanent secretaries on the day before Cabinet meets and ostensibly decides upon issues.

My time in the Cabinet Office had also entailed a close working relationship with people in No. 10. Besides the Prime Minister, with whom I had occasional and 'unofficial' meetings on government business, I met principally with Alastair Campbell and James Purnell. James and another No. 10 adviser, Liz Lloyd, were friends of Tim Allen from schooldays and had been recruited to join the No. 10 team. Products of that vanguardist source of young socialists, Guildford Grammar School, they did not sit easily in my political world.

I recall on one occasion Ms Lloyd representing No. 10 at a Cabinet committee reviewing drinking laws. At one point, she felt inspired to dream aloud of a 'café' society in all of our towns and cities. I was highly amused by this almost utopian, but wholly misplaced, vision of the kind of change which might be imposed on our pub culture. I feared that this was New Labour made flesh – trite and unrealistic.

James came to represent much of what the Mandelsons of this world saw as the future of the Labour Party. Bright and energetic, he was also devoid of experience of politics and of life; yet like his colleagues in No. 10, he probably had more influence on government policy than many Cabinet ministers. It was simple enough for people like James – he just said that 'No. 10 wants such and such' and generally ministers and departments complied. The assumption was that 'No. 10' was a synonym for the Prime Minister. Of course, it was not; but if the Prime Minister had no dialogue with some of his Cabinet members, it was hardly surprising if ministers took no chances.

I dealt with Alastair over the establishment of the Strategic Communications Unit. My involvement was based on our departmental responsibility for cross-government initiatives, and the fact that one of my agencies was the Central Office of Information – the government's official propaganda arm. I found Alastair very easy to work with and extremely focussed on ensuring that a cohesive message came out of government. It was little wonder that Blair became more and more reliant on his counsel.

Mind you, this varied away from Alastair's formal responsibilities as a special adviser, although one with powers over civil servants. Two examples spring to mind of when he exercised his discretion about his boss's non-governmental activities. When he did get involved, there was an inevitable spin on matters.

The Blairs were in the Seychelles on holiday when reports came in of Tony's heroic rescue of a drowning man. It was Charlie Falconer who put me straight: actually, Blair had been on a mobile phone when the 'rescue' occurred. Apparently, whilst out in a boat, Blair neared a German tourist swimming off one of the islands and offered him a ride back to shore, although the swimmer was in no difficulties. Alastair transmuted this into a feat of derring-do for our willing and gullible newspapers.

Alastair was wiser to steer clear of another Blair family event, one with all of the possibilities of a presentational disaster. Cherie Blair's father, Tony Booth, was to marry yet again, having detached himself from his Canadian partner. His daughter rang me and asked if I could arrange a wedding ceremony for them in a church in my constituency where the parish priest, a friend of mine, was her cousin. I was very worried about this.

Cherie was understandably paranoid about publicity. It had to be done in strictest privacy, and that would be tricky. We eventually settled on a date for the 'wedding', on a Friday, immediately after the end of the annual conference in Blackpool. The civil service would be held later in Derbyshire, but they were insistent on a church ceremony.

This was always going to problematic. The priest in question, Father John Thompson, was a delightful man and a dutiful priest, but he had courted controversy before when he had blessed Tony Booth's marriage to soap star Pat Phoenix. The Catholic Church does not remarry divorcees, and many saw little distinction between a formal wedding service and a customised 'blessing' of the participants. I wanted no part of the travesty of a nuptial mass or service.

I checked with John whether or not he had the archbishop's agreement to do it. Despite the archbishop being in Rome, he insisted that everything was approved. As if to convince me, he went through the service with me. In truth, I saw little difference between what he proposed and the normal wedding service, although I do not claim to be a canonical expert.

On the day, we succeeded in keeping the lid on things. To my surprise, all but one of Tony's children by his various liaisons turned up for the ceremony, as did the children of the various marriages of Stephanie, the bride-to-be. Having gathered everyone in the church, we locked the doors. I was terrified that a journalist would get in. The only outsiders were the Prime Minister's bodyguard detail.

As John donned his vestments in the vestry, Ian, the senior bodyguard, was loading bullets into his gun. A grinning Tony bounded in to chat to me about nothing in particular when there was a loud knock on the outside vestry door. I opened the door and there, to my dismay, stood the local stringer for the *Daily Mirror*, Frank Corless. What he made of the priest, protector and Prime

Minister behind me, I can only guess. I begged him to keep this to himself for half an hour or so and I would get him an exclusive with Blair. He agreed to this and I relocked the door.

The ceremony began with me still very anxious that there was no photographer or scribbler in the church. The two readers of the lessons were the Prime Minister and myself. Then we reached the facsimile of the wedding rite. At one point, John said: 'And do you, Tony, take this woman Stephanie, as your wife, for richer for poorer, in sickness and in health, till death do you part... [pause] again?' At this, the Prime Minister nearly collapsed in fits of suppressed laughter, trying to hide himself behind one of the huge pillars in the church. I must confess that I felt exactly the same way. What Alastair would have made of it all I do not know. I assume that he had just washed his hands of it, given that Blair had told me he had not wanted to attend, but Cherie had insisted. Alastair, of course, also famously remarked that 'we do not do God'.

Once I took up my new post as the under-secretary of state for Defence, I threw myself into the job with gusto. My colleagues were George Robertson, John Spellar and Liz Symons. This was a very right-wing collection of ministers. George I believed to be overrated. He had seemed to me a courtier in John Smith's day, and all I thought he brought to the table was a loyalty to whoever happened to be leader. More remarkable was to see him nod off during briefings. Perhaps I had an unbalanced view because before very long, he was to leave the MoD to become secretary general of NATO. It could be that, knowing of his future, he had lost interest.

Whether that was true or not, he still made the Defence report to the annual conference in 1999. He was very upset with me because I did not sit at the front of the MPs section whilst he made his speech. Presumably, he believed that I ought to have been some kind of cheerleader for him at his swansong. That was not me. The courtier approach to politics is alive and well in the United Kingdom – just go to Westminster and it is blindingly apparent. It remains to many the ladder to promotion. To me, it is demeaning to the individual concerned and to the office held. I was not persuaded of George's case. He left after Conference, anyway, to be replaced by Geoff Hoon.

Spellar was – and is – a consummate political operator. Totally lacking in social skills, he is, nevertheless, a workaholic totally immersed in politics. So obsessive was he that he volunteered to be the minister on call across the whole Christmas–New Year period of 1999–2000, when such dire things were predicted of the so-called millennium bug. Frankly, I was far happier with my family.

Liz Symons took over the role of procurement minister in Defence. Huge sums are spent – and wasted – in procurement. Her predecessor had been the illustrious Lord Gilbert, who had picked up the reins in 1997 of the job he had relinquished in the Labour defeat of 1979. Liz was the former leader of the elite trade union for mandarins, the First Division Association. Her partner, Phil Bassett, a former journalist from Merseyside, was yet another of No. 10's special advisers.

Once again, I was afforded a huge office, complete with en-suite bathroom, and an excellent team of private office staff. My diary was stuffed to overflowing – most of it, as it transpired, meaningless – and I was given a very long list of overseas trips from which I could choose. Naturally, the object was to keep meddlesome ministers from becoming too involved in the running of a department. Easier to fill up their days with irrelevances than anything of substance.

The MoD was an amazing place, at that time scheduled for refurbishment. Its canteen, located in the bowels of the building, was like something from the Minitruth in *Nineteen Eighty-Four*.

Far below that was the bunker. This was the nuclear bomb-proof redoubt from where war – even nuclear war – could be fought. I recall marvelling at the huge, thick steel doors at its entrance, listening to a general describe how they could withstand a direct hit by a nuclear bomb. I remarked that I would sooner take my chances on the surface with my family. In all seriousness, the general said: 'Ministers would need to be down here, to give the orders.' So much for the military mindset, which was beyond my ken. Familiarising myself with the department, I visited the press office. The main office was what I expected – reasonably fit for purpose with regular press officers. Then I discovered that each of the three services had their own press office nearby, staffed by officers. Further investigation revealed scores, indeed, hundreds, of press officers scattered around the country. Unfortunately, they were based where the services were, rather than close to the media. Thus, an army base in, say, Much Marching, might well have a press officer presence, but there was nothing in major media centres like Newcastle, Manchester or Birmingham. It was a huge waste of a resource.

What can one expect of an organisation which places more stress on uniforms than on accommodation? I was fascinated to observe the different uniforms worn by the Chief of the Defence Staff. He might don three or four different outfits in a day, depending on where he was going, or whom he might be visiting. Meanwhile, squaddies were living in slums, whilst the best housing formerly owned by the MoD had been flogged off to a Japanese bank. Worse still, the housing had to be upgraded before handover, leaving even fewer resources for housing poor Tommy Atkins.

There was, like in Whitehall, different cultures in different services. The Royal Air Force saw itself as more egalitarian and professional than the others, but that did not always sink in with the MoD. My otherwise dutiful office kept from me messages from Air Marshal Sir Christopher Colville. They were unaware that I had known Chris as a boy. In fact, my mother looked after him and his brother when their own mother died. Chris was true to the Air Force's meritocratic nature. He had risen from air cadet to the NATO No. 2 spot. Not bad for a Scouser.

The navy, of course, insisted that it remained the 'Senior Service' but with its own social flexibility. Arriving on HMS *Ocean* by helicopter, I was able to put the captain's face to his name – Ross Lidbetter. His elder brother was an old pal of mine from my youth. Ross played guitar in the carrier's rock band whilst the lead singer was a seaman from Liverpool. Informality ruled in the band, but everyone knew his or her place in the more formal run of things on the ship.

The army, on the other hand, was of a different class, literally and metaphorically. I was always reminded at the MoD of a conversation with Nicholas Soames, another ex-MoD minister, in the Commons' tea room. He announced to no one in particular that if he was colonel of his regiment, and I was the regimental sergeant major, it would be the best fighting unit in the country, if not the world. Going along with his fantasy to a point, I asked Nicholas why he could not be the RSM and me the colonel. His look of bewildered incomprehension at the prospect said it all.

Admittedly, much depends on the unit to which one is referring. The Guards are seen as the socially pre-eminent infantry unit. An oik might progress in the engineers or even an unfashionable infantry regiment; but one cannot avoid the class basis of the army, particularly the infantry. Amongst the lower ranks, it is partly explained by the high proportion of recruits who have left one institution, a care home, to join the army, another one. It also partly explains the high proportion of the long-term homeless who are ex-squaddies, unable to cope in civilian life because of their institutionalisation. Their officers, by and large, face no such handicaps in life.

Life in the MoD did have its moments. My travels on departmental business took me to places I would otherwise never have seen. Thus, I dropped in by helicopter to our jungle warfare training camp in the rainforests of Belize. From there, for reasons I never did quite understand, I called in on the new President of Guatemala, Sr Portillo. It took me a little while to figure out who it was he brought to mind. It was the actor Joe Pesci, who had often portrayed psychopaths. No portrayal here – Portillo was the real thing.

Wholly different were trips to Athens and Egypt. Like many people, I am fascinated by the history of the ancient world. It was, therefore, a great privilege when the Egyptian military chief, Marshal Tatanwy, made the pyramids site available to me for an exclusive visit. It was incredible to have an army cordon keeping people away, but even more so to enter the Great Pyramid of Cheops and finding it, well, silent as the grave.

In Athens, the Greek government extended to me a similar privilege. It was easy to understand ministers becoming addicted to such a lifestyle. The Acropolis was kept closed for my private visit, accompanied by a British expert to guide me around the Parthenon and Erechtheum. I could even stand looking towards Piraeus, imagining the Long Walls in their heyday. The visit gave me a spiritual uplift only made possible by my status as a British defence minister.

Not that all visits were so agreeable. At one stage, I was sent off to assess the dreadful conflict in Sierra Leone. En route, I was to make an official visit to Nigeria. Arriving in a small Queen's Flight aircraft, I was met by our new high commissioner to Nigeria, who had transferred from his last post as an ambassador to Indonesia.

Whilst there I had to call on the Nigerian Defence Minister, General Danjuma. To the mystification of officials, the general said he recognised my name. It was because of my brother, I reminded him, before we got down to business. Afterwards, the high commissioner asked me what the general and I were on about. I explained that I had a brother who had been in Nigeria working for an American company, of which he was a director, for about twenty-five years. Danjuma, corrupt, like many senior Nigerians, had tried to take over the company. When he failed, he ordered a 'hit' on my brother to send a message to the firm. As it happened, when his men shot up my brother's car, he was not in it. However, his wife, over on holiday from their home in Texas, was. They shot her through both legs, crippling her for life. This was at the orders of the man I met that day. Again, such is politics.

On I flew to Sierra Leone. It was surreal. My close protection squad and I were dropped off at the deserted and devastated Lungi airport. Our Queen's Flight plane immediately flew out to Dakar – it was too dangerous for it to stay at Lungi. We were met by a squad of mercenaries who took us to a huge old Russian helicopter, crewed by Ukrainians. This flew us into a fortress in the centre of Freetown. Like a scene from *Apocalypse Now*, the mercenaries were machine-gunning rebel positions below. It was a hairy, if short, flight.

My host, a 'Sanders of the River' type, was the British high commissioner, Peter Penfold. Locals had taken him to their hearts to such an extent that they carried him around in a sedan chair. He was not to the Foreign Office's liking, but I stayed with him at his shot-up residence. My close protection squad mounted an all-night vigil so that I might sleep. It was not so easy with trip wires for stun grenades stretched out across the approach to my room.

I met with the leaders of the various factions and the

American-installed President. I was particularly interested in the two rebel leaders, Johnny Paul Koroma and Foday Sankoh. The former had been captured at one stage by the latter and buried up to his neck for two days. Inexplicably, he was then set free. Sankoh was undoubtedly the worse of the two. He was accompanied everywhere by an ally and bodyguard known as General Mosquito, who wore ammunition bandoliers like a bit part player in a Mexican movie. Koroma's people were like a West African version of Haiti's Ton Ton Macoute, complete with flash, cheap jewellery and fake designer T-shirts. Without a doubt, ridding the country of such hideous people would be an entirely justifiable war.

Sierra Leone had been the jewel in the west African crown as the winds of change blew through the old British Empire. It was held up as a model for others to emulate. Nothing exemplified its sophistication at the time more than Fourah Bay College. Perhaps the fact that Leo Blair had once taught there explained Tony Blair's great interest in the small, but beautiful, former British colony.

eight

If the sum total of politics was a place on the ladder of government, with prospects and perks and overseas jollies, then I was on course for satisfaction of a high order. However, there are other dimensions to being a member of Parliament, like the health and shape of one's party, and – most importantly – the wellbeing of constituents. Both of these had given me concerns since the advent of 'New' Labour in 1994.

Prior to accession to office in 1997, shadow frontbenchers had spent weekends at Templeton College, Oxford, in an attempt to learn some of the skills required of an actual minister. After our long years of opposition, only a small handful of our number had any experience of government, and then at only a junior level. It was a sensible attempt to prepare us for the unknown, and one of the texts we used was *How to Be a Minister* by Gerald Kaufman.

In that book, Gerald wisely warned of the twin perils facing a new and inexperienced minister, which he called 'ministerialitis' and 'departmentalitis'. The former was a euphemism for ego, where ministers become preoccupied with their new status rather than what can be done with the position. Similarly, those suffering from departmentalitis become obsessed with the department's (i.e. mandarins') agenda, forgetting their own political exigencies. Almost from the first day, I had seen examples of these amongst colleagues who had forgotten Gerald's forewarnings, or had never taken them in the first place.

Thus, even in our early days, Gordon Brown was plotting his political future in No. 11 whilst the country awaited and expected radical change. His response was to stick to the previous government's spending commitments for two years, whilst inviting party members from around the country to his carefully staged receptions. Other, lesser, mortals seemed to grow a couple of inches within days of taking office, almost physically distancing themselves when in the Commons from the backbench hoi polloi.

It was evident in the many committees I attended. One such is known as the Legislation Committee. It is charged with examining legislation and prioritising it for consideration in one house or other in Parliament. The very first issue we dealt with was a short bill to allow the new Lord Chancellor, Derry Irvine, to have the permanent secretary of his choice, and this required a change in the law. As approval was sought from each committee member, I said that the Cabinet Office supported it, but added, in humour, that I thought it was a job creation project for impecunious lawyers (Derry wanted a lawyer friend in the post). It was like abusing the Pope in a conclave, going down like a lead balloon before so many people taking themselves even more seriously than they had done when on the opposition front bench.

On another occasion, I suggested that the Prime Minister ought to meet with junior ministers, and put my idea in a note to the then chief whip, Nick Brown. When I heard nothing back, I sent him another polite note, with a copy of the first missive. I eventually received a pompous response which said: 'I told you that I will consider your request [he had told me nothing of the sort], and I will.' I never heard from Brown again on the matter.

Far worse was the personal demeanour of many ministerial colleagues who affected superior airs and graces. They tended to mix only with other ministers or their personal circle of courtiers. I found this hubristic project of their sense of their own importance profoundly depressing.

Within departments, there had been early hesitation in some and frenetic activity in others. Admittedly, underneath the rhetoric, there was no truly radical programme to implement. There was logic in bedding down as a government and familiarising ourselves with not just being in government, but also having a massive parliamentary majority. So ingrained was the caution that the new Prime Minister maintained his dialogue with the Liberal Democrats. I could not decide whether the extent of our victory had not sunk in with him, or whether he still aspired to a straightforward union of the two parties.

As the months of government turned into years, the lack of ambition in government confounded me. Much of what we did was simply a continuation of what had obtained under Thatcher and Major. Like many, within and without government, I awaited some sign that the leadership was to break from its complacent self-satisfaction with being in office and strike out in a new political direction, more consonant with traditional Labour values and policies. That change never arrived. Instead, it became more and more obvious that just being there was sufficient for the leadership. The kind of social change which I and others sought was not in its political lexicon.

Their language talked of the needs of 'the City' and 'deregulation'. 'Privatisation' was repeatedly threatened, and 'private finance' advocated at every turn in preference to state funding. The trade unions were never mentioned, other than in a negative way, castigated as obstacles to the much-mooted yet amorphous 'reform' of the public sector. I began to believe I was no longer in the Labour Party.

The change within the party was exemplified in a debate at a party conference on New Labour. Mandelson was extolling the virtues of the rebrand to a crowded hall whilst I was trying to pin down what it actually signified. An exasperated Ben Bradshaw had a go at me from the back of the crowd, saying: 'That is the trouble with people like you, Peter. You just do not understand. You cannot define New Labour; it is something you feel rather than articulate.' It seemed as if I was at a religious revivalist meeting, rather than at a party political debate. Truly, I was a long way adrift from the New Labour zealot.

Matters came to a head at a dinner with Mo Mowlam. Mo's husband Jon, my wife Bernie, journalist Tony Bevins and I were dining in Mo's apartment in Admiralty Buildings. As the wine flowed I became more and more critical of the government's direction. Mo, being a straight talker, challenged me directly: 'Well, if you are that pissed off, don't complain to me. Resign.' That very weekend, having discussed it with my wife, I resolved to take her advice.

I did not wish to cause a fuss; for all its blandness, it was still a Labour government, and I wished it well. I just realised that I had nothing in common with it in my thinking. I would be living and working a lie if I stayed put. Nevertheless, I was determined to go out quietly. It was also the case that, if I was not careful, political practitioners of the dark arts would rubbish me before I resigned if they got wind of my going.

Knowing that the Monday newspapers 'went to bed' at about 6.30 on Sunday evenings, I gave an exclusive on my resignation to Tom Baldwin of the *Times*. That meant that my embargoed statement would be published first, anodyne as it was, and hopefully it would set the mood for coverage. At 6.30 p.m., I faxed my resignation directly to No. 10. Within minutes, I had both Tony Blair and Alastair Campbell on the telephone. Alastair made a comment about my timing, which I chose to take as a back-handed compliment. The Prime Minister, on the other hand, mumbled a half-hearted request that I change my mind. Too late, I told him, and that was it.

I was inundated with calls and faxes (emails were not my forte) from journalists wanting to speak with me. Some even came to my home, but I kept my silence. My statement said all that I needed to say, that I wanted to do more for and in my constituency. To avoid a media ambush, I stayed away from London on the Monday, going down on the Tuesday. I had arranged to meet Charlie Falconer for dinner in the Lords and I kept my commitment, meeting him in the Lords' Dining Room.

Charlie was too cute to tackle me head on over my resignation. Besides, he was visibly puzzled by the stream of members of the Lords coming over to congratulate me on resigning and shaking my hand. He was shocked when, after dinner, we went into the Strangers' Bar. It was crowded and gave a great roar of greeting as we entered, followed by a chorus of 'For He's a Jolly Good Fellow'. I had not realised how many others felt concerns about the government similar to mine.

It did not seem appropriate, however, to create an unnecessary stir. Unwittingly, I think I still hoped that the government would become more proactive for our traditional supporters. I resolved to keep my head down until the novelty of my resignation wore off. That way my loyalty would not be questioned, either.

When I did eventually break my vow of silence, it was after a Budget speech by Gordon Brown. He gave old age pensioners a 75p rise in that Budget and I was appalled. Each day we were seeing reports of the rich getting richer – in part thanks to the Chancellor's largesse – and here we were actually insulting pensioners with a miserly increase. I rose in the chamber and said so.

Needless to say, the Chancellor did not take kindly to my criticism and told me so later in the tea room. We had what is sometimes called 'a free and friendly exchange of views'. Brown challenged me over my claimant-heavy constituency, and I replied that I had ideas. He invited me to come and share those ideas with him. I quickly agreed. It was not to be that straightforward, however.

I suggested a meeting with the Chancellor and some private sector big hitters, to see how they would deal with an area generally agreed to be one of the most deprived in the country. Furthermore, the local council had shown itself to be institutionally incapable of addressing the complex issues bedevilling north Liverpool. Brown agreed, but he wanted first to see a list of those who might be invited. I took a list to him. Reading it he said: 'You won't get these people'.

'I already have,' I replied. 'All they want is a date.'

He could not, or would not, believe that I had contacts with senior City people as well as the local great and good. Reluctantly, he agreed to the meeting in No. 11.

Our guests arrived on the day promptly and eager to help. The plan was that the Chancellor would chair the meeting, I would make a short presentation on the problems of north Liverpool, and then we would tap into the collective wit of our invitees. To my amazement, Brown began by challenging me over my opposition to workfare. He presumably had decided to take the opportunity to show these captains of commerce that he was tough on the feckless and work-shy poor. It was weak characters like me who stood in his way.

The meeting was not a great success. Brown had made his point and showed little interest in pulling people together in support of north Liverpool. Attendees commented to me on it and I was dismayed. I took the view then that, politically, he was beyond redemption. As the Prime Minister had gone off in one direction, so the other half of the ruling diarchy, the Chancellor, was going off in another. Neither of their takes on the government's direction was of any comfort to me. Fortunately, it seemed psephologically impossible that we could lose our second election. We did not lose, of course; we had another huge majority. The question was: what would we do with it? The answer came later that year.

George W. Bush had become US President by highly dubious means; yet he was duly sworn in to succeed Bill Clinton. A man of little grace, and great political ignorance, he headed up the most right-wing American administration in decades. Within months, Bush had made radical changes to American policy, altering its military strategy, revoking the long-standing ABM treaty with Russia and committing billions of dollars to missile defence – Star Wars II, as it was known. Then came 9/11, when groups of Islamic terrorists took over four American passenger jets, slamming them into the World Trade Center in New York, the Pentagon near Washington DC and a field in Pennsylvania.

These attacks were the latest organised through the al-Qaeda Islamist organisation, based in Afghanistan. They shook the United States and the whole world to the core. For some days, near panic took hold, as expectations of more terror attacks grew. There was also a fear about the nature of the inevitable American response to these attacks, the most significant on the United States since Pearl Harbor.

Credit should be given to Tony Blair that he seemed to grasp very early on that a wounded America could be a dangerous entity if left to its own devices. He was immediate in his expressions of British solidarity with the United States in its time of need. He flew to New York to bear witness in person to the great loss of life there. For me, it was the apogee of his time as Prime Minister, as he found the words of which President Bush was incapable.

As he set off from London to build a 'coalition of the willing' against this terrorism, I was one of those who wished him well in the Commons, although the *Times* described me as a discordant voice. My dissonance concerned a reference to 'intelligence sources' by the Prime Minister. I had never put much faith in spooks. My views were reinforced by my own intelligence briefings when I joined the MoD. As I signed my life away, three spooks shared their secrets with me. As they finished, two left and the one remaining told me of matters on a need-to-know basis. Then he left, one of the other two replaced him and the process was repeated. Finally, the second left and the third returned to tell me *his* particular secrets. I found it a joke, particularly when I endured the same pantomime with two other groups of spooks. How clever are this lot, I thought, when they cannot trust each other? My low opinion was further reinforced by the constant refrain from senior officers that the importance of the so-called 'special relationship' was in the willingness of the Americans to share information. This highly dubious assertion was to be tested to breaking point in the years to come.

Blair could not be denied support in his early post-9/11 endeavours, however. The problem lay in the fact that those early months were emotionally charged with so much hyperbole that it was difficult to have a rational conversation. In turn, when American bombers and cruise missiles began to rain down on Taliban-controlled Afghanistan, it was very hard to object; or, if you did, to get a hearing. In America, the dogs of war were unleashed, but targeted at more than the al-Qaeda bases in Afghanistan. The neo-cons who populated the Bush administration had other targets in mind, shared with Israel: Syria, Iran and Iraq. Bush himself had a personal grudge with the Iraqi President, Saddam Hussein, who had tried to assassinate Bush Sr. His acolytes saw political and commercial advantages in taking out the Iraqi regime, and it quickly became the focus of their attention.

The question in the United Kingdom, which is still being asked, is: how did Blair become so wrapped up in this crusade against Saddam? Others will answer that more fully in the course of time. Suffice to say that Blair committed himself to an attack on Iraq, and that was to split party, Parliament and people. It led to him becoming an incredibly divisive figure in the United Kingdom, whilst being lauded elsewhere.

I was wholly unconvinced throughout the long build-up to the final Commons debate and during the actual onslaught on Iraq. In some ways, it was a peculiar period as individuals took up their positions and argued in the tea rooms and bars about everything from weapons of mass destruction to legality to our allegiance to the United States. It was not as if there were no other issues, but Iraq came to dominate all else. It divided friends and united former enemies in a cause. It is worth recalling that the official opposition was, in some respects, more bellicose than the government towards

Iraq. It certainly gave Blair a degree of certitude about the likely political support when the debate metamorphosed into the inevitable military action.

Life could be so unreal. On one occasion I was called in to see the Prime Minister. Prior to this, various feelers had been put to me to rejoin the government, which I had ignored. It was standard practice to try to assimilate critics into the government fold. On this occasion, I spent over an hour in the garden of No. 10, with Blair, as his little son Leo played in the background. Superficially at least, he wanted to sound me out on the state of politics at that time. Before long, he turned to my own situation, asking me to come on board with the government. There was a job for me to do, he said, and I could, of course, carry on writing and saying the things which I was already doing.

This was absurd and I told him so: 'If I continued to say and write what I believe, you would have to sack me. In that case, you would look a fool for having taken me back in, and I would look a fool for having agreed to go back in.'

We agreed to disagree, and, as I left, his last words to me were to think it over. He still believed that there was a job for me to do in government. I have sometimes wondered what, if anything, he actually had in mind.

When the great debate on Iraq was held, I had written a rather simple amendment, saying that the case for war was unproven, but wishing our troops a swift resolution if it were to come to war. There were other amendments being touted around, but they were either too complex or too argumentative. We needed to rally as many votes against the war as possible, so the necessary amendment had to be widely acceptable.

On the day of the debate, I went to see Mr Speaker, Michael

Martin, putting it to him that, as the Liberal Democrat amendment had been accepted by him in the last debate on Iraq, it was surely the turn of rebel Labour backbenchers – much larger in number than the Liberal Democrats – to have their amendment (i.e. mine) accepted. He made no formal commitment, but as I took my seat in the chamber that afternoon, he sent a note to me saying that he had selected our amendment and would be calling on me to propose it. This was daunting, as I was unprepared. I had expected the Speaker, if he called anyone, to turn to a former Cabinet member like Chris Smith to do the honours. I also realised that the Prime Minister and the leader of the opposition had as much time as they needed to set out their case, whilst I had only the backbencher's abbreviated allocation of eight minutes.

I did my best, following on from marathon speeches by the two leaders, and the debate continued throughout the day. After my own contribution, I went to the tea room for a coffee. To my surprise, the Prime Minister made a rare appearance there. He approached me and said: 'Well, Peter, I suppose it's too late to get you to change your mind?'

'Definitely,' I answered. 'Sit down and have a cigarette.'

'You know I don't smoke,' he smiled.

'I know, but you look as if your nerves would be settled by one.'

Later on, he got the parliamentary majority which he craved, but it was never to give his actions the legitimacy required. He was to be forever tainted by his determination to stand side by side with George Bush in toppling Saddam.

Three members of his government resigned over the war: Robin Cook, John Denham and Lord Hunt. Robin Cook, acknowledged as a first-rate debater, made a devastating critique of the government's policy on Iraq in his resignation speech. However, unlike many commentators, I remain unconvinced that this was solely an issue of high principle. I have always suspected that Cook's resignation was at least, in part, a political decision to put himself at the head of the internal opposition within the Labour Party.

He had, after all, been demoted from Foreign Secretary to Leader of the House. He also knew that Brown was his implacable foe. There was one occasion in the chamber when he appeared to see that there was no longer-term future in the government for him. In the course of a statement to the House, he was attacked head on by Jack Cunningham and Gerald Kaufman. Both of these old right-wing battlers had sized up Cook's vulnerability and went for him, no doubt in part as a payback for Cook's razor-sharp barbs in the past. It was logical for Cook, therefore, to set himself as the rallying point for backbench dissent.

On the night of his resignation, I was rather more impressed by the quiet dignity of John Denham in his resignation speech. Eventually, he was to become a member of the Cabinet; but, on that night, he was not to know that. He was genuinely giving away a promising career in government in order to follow his conscience.

One of the early casualties was Clare Short, of course. Bizarrely, she voted with the government for the war and then resigned afterwards. The more she spoke, the more confusing became her position and the more confused her audience. Despite her subsequent trenchant criticism of government policy in Iraq, no one took her seriously again. A long career in the front line of politics simply fizzled out.

On the night of the vote, there was a tremendous amount of activity, with many attempts to dissuade dissidents from voting against the government. It was not as if the government would be denied a majority in the House. With official Conservative support, it was not remotely possible. Yet a large vote against the government would create its own political problems. Whilst nobody tried to persuade me on that evening, it was apparent that pressure was being brought to bear on many members of the PLP. Some of the usual bribery took place – offers of inconsequential jobs can work wonders. There were also the threats – not so much about the future of the government, but more the future of the individual member concerned, particularly if he or she held a marginal seat. There is nothing like political survival to motivate many of my colleagues. The only discordant note was a torrent of abuse towards me from neighbouring MP Jane Kennedy as I left the 'No' lobby on the government's motion. I was mad about this, as I had known Jane for so long; and, to my knowledge, I had never done her other than favours. I suspected that she, like others involved with Labour Friends of Israel, was being pressurised in turn to deliver the 'right' result.

The campaign against this horrific war did not end with that vote. It went on and on as the woeful neglect of post-invasion plans became apparent. It suited a wide variety of people, from George Galloway to the Socialist Workers Party, who manipulated their Stop the War Coalition very successfully. It did not suit those who simply sought peace, least of all the Iraqi people who died in their thousands. All of the way through this protracted carnage, Blair insisted that the course being followed was the right one. There were strong hints that 'the gentleman is not for turning'.

At one stage, an old Australian friend, Jim Bacon, Premier of Tasmania, came to London. He and his wife Honey were desperate to visit No. 10, so Fraser Kemp and I set out to arrange it. Entering the reception area inside No. 10, the Bacons got more than they anticipated. The Prime Minister came out to say hello and to have his picture taken with them. Blair then decided, despite protocol, to give them an impromptu tour of the building. As we went into the Cabinet room, there was a cluster of people waiting outside, including Jack Straw, Geoff Hoon, the Chief of Defence Staff and the American ambassador. The looks on the faces of Straw and Hoon, in particular, were a delight. I imagine they were wondering what I was doing in there with the Prime Minister and two tanned strangers.

No doubt this particular heavyweight get-together was one of the many meetings convened to ensure a 'successful' war. That outcome was increasingly unlikely in presentational terms, as the bloodshed carried on and the myth of weapons of mass destruction was finally laid to rest. The disastrous Iraq War became the yardstick by which Blair's second spell as Prime Minister was judged. Surprisingly, his lieutenants in this exercise seemed relatively untouched by it. Gordon Brown made only one reference to Iraq prior to the great debate, but, as Chancellor, he was paymaster for the war. Jack Straw was, after Blair, the principal apologist for this criminal endeavour. Geoff Hoon, as Secretary of State for Defence, was metaphorically in the front line of the prosecution of the war. Interestingly, given the illegal nature of the conflict, Blair, Straw and Hoon were all lawyers. They above anyone should have been aware of the legal quicksands upon which they stood.

To this day, I ask why, if so many could see through the implausibility and superficiality of the government's case, why could not those at the top? Was it that they chose not to see? Were they so blinded by peripheral issues, like the mythical 'special relationship', that their judgement went away? Were they misled by intelligence which turned out to be rather unintelligent? To me, it is straightforward. Either they did not see the incongruity of the government's case – in which case they were, and are, unfit to hold high office – or they deliberately chose to be party to the deception of Parliament and to an illegal war.

nine

Prior to the 2001 election, I recall a telephone call from Alastair Campbell. I was having a drink on the House of Commons terrace at the time with Charlie Falconer. Alastair asked me what I thought of the state of play for the government. Naturally and honestly, I told him that I believed that the government had a fair wind of public support behind it.

Furthermore, it was inconceivable that, come the election, the Labour government would fail to harvest the majority support of the British people for a further term of office. It appeared to me to be psephologically impossible for us not to be returned. However, I remarked to Alastair, the real judgement on Labour would come in the election after that.

As it happened, the 2001 election came and went, and Labour

was predictably returned with another huge majority. The Tories were still seen as the nasty party and had made no discernible impact upon the electorate's view of what was in the nation's interest. Moreover, Blair's personal ratings were still extremely high, and that was a bonus to us all. Then came the events of September 11 2001.

I remember the day clearly. I was in my family home, where I had turned on the television to watch Blair speak to the Trades Union Congress annual bash. I had a particular interest because I was to attend and speak at it the following day. I was amazed to see the scheduled coverage switch to cover the unfolding drama in the United States, and also watched as Blair cut short his visit to the brothers – and his speech – and headed back to London.

It was a significant day in many respects. For example, I heard live from New York my old friend Ian Williams giving the BBC an on-the-spot account via telephone of the chaos in Manhattan. Blair, of course, was to take a stance which would be the hallmark of the remainder of his time in office, standing 'shoulder to shoulder' with our trans-Atlantic cousins in their hour of need. This was possibly his finest hour – yet it was not long before it went wrong.

Having recalled Parliament for an emergency session, he flew off to the United States to pledge our support in seeking the perpetrators of the attacks on American soil. He went with the overwhelming support of Parliament and people, although the *Times* described me as a discordant voice for querying the reliability of the intelligence which suddenly began to be bandied about.

It became clear very quickly that the American neo-cons who peopled the Bush Administration were keen to exploit the tragedy of 9/11 for their own ideological purposes. Although the adherents of al-Qaeda, based in the mountains of Afghanistan, were responsible for the terrorist attacks, the Republican political machine fixed its gaze on an 'axis of evil' – Iran, Iraq and North Korea, with lesser enemies like Syria and Libya in the background.

This was the genesis of eighteen months of increasingly acrimonious debate over a growing determination to pursue an agenda devised in Washington and Jerusalem, but supported by the British government and the official opposition, the Conservative Party. Large numbers of Labour members of Parliament, the Liberal Democrats and the nationalists grew ever more strident in their opposition to the increasingly bellicose arguments of government spokesmen and their supporters in Parliament and in the press.

The end result was our participation in an illegal and immoral war, launched on the basis of a false premise. The court of public opinion has, in my view, condemned Blair for this, although he has faced no formal jury. Nevertheless, the war was without doubt the dominant feature of his second term as Prime Minister; and I had felt sure that he, and, by extension, the Labour Party, would suffer heavily for his folly at the next general election.

When that came in 2005, there was a great deal of trepidation in the Labour camp. The effect on the leadership was striking, as I saw for myself during the campaign.

I had a call from Wayne Swan, shadow treasurer in the Australian parliament. He was an old friend and he was in a pickle. He told me that had been stitched up on his visit to London by the conservative Australian government of John Howard. All organisational and logistical support for the visit, usually provided by the Australian high commission, had been withdrawn. Scheduled meetings were cancelled, and there was a fear that he might be portrayed as on a work-free freebie trip to London at the expense of the Australian taxpayer.

Through Sue Nye, I arranged to take Wayne to our party campaign headquarters in Victoria Street. There, I would take some photos of Wayne with the Chancellor, for transmission to the Australian media. As it happened, Blair was also there, and I took snaps of Wayne with each of them and the three of them together. It did the trick Down Under.

Yet what struck me was the gaunt look of Blair. He looked old, grey and worn. Brown, on the other hand, looked perfectly relaxed, even deferring to Blair when it was just the four of us together. Perhaps Brown knew something the rest of us did not. The headquarters itself was full of Cabinet members and hangers on. I wondered why they were there, rather than out campaigning. I assumed it was because the latter could be exhausting work and there was no career advantage in being elsewhere.

When the results came in, we had lost seats. Being mindful of my long-ago prediction to Alastair Campbell, we had been held to account, although to my surprise we still ended up with a reasonable majority. This was in spite of what I had believed to be a largely negative public in terms of Iraq. Of course, the infamous vagaries of our voting system also came into play. Despite only receiving around 35 per cent of the popular vote we had a clear working majority; but the portents for a future election were clear.

For Blair personally, it was undoubtedly a matter of great pride that, as party leader, he had led us to a third election victory on the trot. We knew, however, that winning government on the basis of the votes of only a third of the electorate, was not a sustainable position. As a party, we needed to move on from the New Labour branding that had largely been a presentation of the party as a projection of the Blairite personality cult.

Needless to say, the matter arose at the first meeting in the new parliament of the Parliamentary Labour Party. I was the second person called to speak, and I was blunt in my comments. Addressing the Prime Minister, I told him that I believed it was time for him to go and that he should go quickly. Turning to his self-styled successor, Brown, I remarked that he was no dauphin. There must, I argued, be an election for the next leader, whoever it might be, and not a shoo-in.

Blair was not one to go easily. He tried to hang on, and succeeded for two years, but realised eventually that politics had moved on and so must he. This led to the quest for a new leader. Brown was the odds-on pretender to the leadership, but the Labour Party has rules and these had to be observed. This meant that any candidates for leader needed a minimum threshold number of nominations to go on the ballot paper. This was where Brown's long-term planning and ruthlessness bore fruit. For there was no viable opponent able to muster sufficient nominations.

John McDonnell of the Campaign Group had tried hard to rally enough support but failed to do so. I was approached on his behalf, but I was no more enamoured of his hard left approach than I would be of a hard right one. At one stage, Michael Meacher tried to launch himself as an alternative candidate and was quite miffed when I would have nothing to do with his fantasy. In fact, I remained as one of the small number – less than a dozen in total – who refused to nominate anyone at all. Overwhelmingly, the members of the Parliamentary Labour Party nominated Brown, including virtually all those who have since plotted and schemed to overthrow his leadership. Brown's only critic of note to have refused to nominate anyone was Charles Clarke.

Subsequent to Brown having been 'elected' nem. con., I chanced upon a conspiratorial little group, lost in conversation in a corridor. It consisted of Charles Clarke, Stephen Byers and Alan Milburn.

They were muttering away about what a failure Brown was as Prime Minister. I pointed out to Milburn and Byers that they, unlike Clarke, had nominated Brown. They had no cogent answer.

Thus, Brown had become leader without a contest and without the stamp of political legitimacy. Oh, he had the majority of members of Parliament, but the membership of the party and its affiliates had no say in the process. Technically, everything had been done by the book; politically, it was a recipe for disaster.

Although I was never a fan or supporter of Brown, I was not sorry to see Blair go. His time had simply run out, although I had some fond memories of his time as leader. On a one-to-one basis, he had generally been fine to me. For example, as the clock was ticking on his premiership late in 2006, I returned to Parliament after major heart surgery. I was called to put a question in PMQs and paid credit to the NHS and the staff who had treated me. He was generous in his response.

After PMQs, he agreed to meet with my surgeon, Aung Oo, who was down in the House on that day as my guest. Blair was a gracious host to Aung and his wife, talking openly about his own heart condition and laughing amiably with me. I thought that perhaps by then he too had come to terms with the inevitability of his stepping down as Prime Minister. *Sic transit gloria mundi.*

When Brown did take over, his ratings rose and his future as Prime Minister looked rosy. However, it was not long before the repressed doubts about his leadership qualities resurfaced. In the autumn of 2007, he went to the brink of calling an election before retreating on the idea. His poll ratings were high and he had encouraged speculation that he would seek an early mandate in his own right as Prime Minister. Any observer of Brown knew that caution would triumph. He has always wanted certainty rather than exposing himself to any risk. That is why, back in 1994, Brown's people were only sounding out support whilst we were already signing people up on behalf of Blair.

Politics is a rough trade, and weakness is quickly spotted and exploited. From this point on, Brown was viewed as a wounded stag at bay. Both press and opposition taunted him. The Blairites, in his Cabinet and on the back benches, plotted and schemed to oust him. The incredible thing is that he managed to stay up and fighting.

This resilience is a positive characteristic of Brown, allied with a steely determination, firstly to be Prime Minister for its own sake and secondly to succeed in the job on his own terms. Years ago, he would have faced real competition for the distinction of being party leader and Prime Minister, but there was no heavyweight division left in Labour politics. Blair had gone, Prescott was finished and Cook was dead. The potential alternative leader, around whom opposition to Brown might coalesce, did not in fact exist.

Protecting his position, Brown filled his Cabinet with people who, whilst often amiable, technically competent and intellectually able, had no politics, no street cred and no experience of life outside a very narrow spectrum. There was little chance of this collection of technocrats and managers taking him on. If nothing else, they have since demonstrated their inability to coordinate a single one of the coups which many of them have tried to undertake. Brown, on the other hand, has been able to dismiss their fumblings as 'froth'. His other internal opponents in the Labour Party, besides a sadly isolated Charles Clarke, wait on events – principally a general election defeat – whilst Brown attempts to determine those events. In this, he has had mixed results.

Despite their long alliance, something of a schism has developed between Brown and Darling. In truth, this is surely in the order of things for any Prime Minister and Chancellor. Whilst Darling has not coveted the top job – indeed, early in Blair's government, he had publicly anticipated retirement – the economic earthquake of the banking crisis and the recession introduced real strains in their long and mutually fruitful cooperation. These strains concerned timing rather than thinking about the necessary corrective actions to meet the exigencies of the crisis. What bothered some of us was their joint failure to cater for the working poor. The catalyst for this concern had been the abolition of the 10 per cent tax rate.

I joined Frank Field and a handful of others in lobbying the Chancellor on this regressive move, but he was not for turning. We tabled an early day motion which gained a good deal of support; and eventually there was to be a vote on an amendment designed to force the hand of the government on the issue.

The whips went into overdrive with the usual mixture of threats, bribery and distortions. Senior ministers were telephoning the hard core dissidents, arguing that our vote – if it eventuated – would not only reject the Budget but would bring down the government. I had two calls on the day in question from Brown himself. He had not spoken to me for years; why he should imagine that I would take any notice of him, I do not know. True to form, there was no dialogue. He simply ranted on with a load of assertions and figures – there was absolutely no opportunity to put a countervailing point of view.

I must admit, however, that I had a sneaking regard for Brown's ability to roll with the punches. Everyday there seemed to be another crisis or disaster, yet he battled on. Unfortunately for him, he obtained little credit for this perseverance. Even his internationally acclaimed efforts in minimising the worst effects of the recession counted for little in the public mind. He came across as a central banker rather than as an inspirational leader.

Yet even amongst his political enemies there were tensions.

I was having a coffee with a colleague on one occasion when we were joined by the Chancellor's long-serving parliamentary private secretary, Ann Coffey, and Jane Kennedy, her close friend and my neighbour. They were discussing dinner arrangements with their good friends Geoff Hoon and Bob Ainsworth. Jane exploded in anger at the mention of the latter, declaring that she would have nothing to do with him.

I assumed this outburst was because of a recently failed plot to bring Brown down. Jane had resigned from government – for the second time – and presumably Bob was supposed to have done the same. Instead, he was promoted, to a Cabinet position. Admittedly, this was less a case of Brown dividing and conquering his enemies than the latter again displaying their ineptitude in getting their act together. Moreover, what had developed over time was an archetypal Labour clash of 'isms' – Brownism versus Blairism – in the mode of Bevanism versus Gaitskellism, but without the real ideological edge of that rivalry of yesteryear. In truth, the modern rivalry was more about personal career aspirations than anything more substantial – more about 'my gang versus your gang'.

It struck me as largely a clash of personalities and styles rather than a clash of ideas, although the principal supporters of each would not say so. Blair's people fall into one broad group, crediting the three election wins of his premiership to his charismatic personality and leadership, almost an affirmation of the *Führerprinzip*. Naturally, no account was taken of the cyclical probability of a Labour win in 1997 with just about any acceptable leader, given the reaction to eighteen years of government by a thoroughly discredited Conservative Party. The Blairites displayed the certainties of the born-again fundamentalist with the devotion of the sectarian towards their leader.

Anyway, the Brownites had a rather different perspective. Their inner core was no less devoted to their leader, despite his glaring lack of charm. Their introspection reflected a more ideologically inclined group, more given to the redistribution of wealth (not so much because it was right in principle, but because it was politically desirable in securing mass support) and less enamoured of the glitzy presentation so beloved of the Blairites. For people like me, this was a fanciful projection of the Brownite faction. They and the Blairites were simply two sides of the same coin in most ways.

Anyway, the personnel often remained the same. Jack Straw had been chairman of Blair's campaign meetings back in 1994 (although I have not a clue what value he added to Blair's candidacy). Then he popped up again as Brown's campaign chairman (for a non-campaign). Jack was never a politician to buck a political opportunity. Blair's *eminence grise*, Mandelson, made a remarkable comeback as Brown's alter ego – not bad for a twice-sacked minister. Mandelson became, to all intents and purposes, the unelected de facto deputy leader in tandem with Brown's unelected leadership. Whilst Harriet Harman was the elected deputy leader, Brown appeared to bypass her completely, preferring to indulge that oleaginous collector of titles, Lord Mandelson.

Other, lesser figures, transferred their allegiance from the Blairite cause to the Brown ascendancy, all, no doubt, in the name of personal advancement. It is not an attractive face of politics when its practitioners do cartwheels to explain their accommodation to political reality in the shape of a new leader. Oddly, however, it was amongst unrecognised backbenchers that there was the most consistent loyalty to Brown. Partly this was down to a detestation of Blair and all of his works amongst members of, say, the Campaign Group. There were also those whose hopes for advancement had been dashed by Blair; but there were some genuine political fans of Brown.

On the other hand, there were those who had been bruised by their encounters down the years with Brown, both in and out of government. He had left a lot of collateral damage behind him. For example, whilst in opposition, the then vibrant Tribune group of backbenchers had produced an alternative economic strategy. This was published in a pamphlet under the joint names of Dr Roger Berry and Peter Hain. The very idea of another line of economic thinking within the party was anathema to Brown. He set out – and succeeded – in the destroying the Tribune group as an active political force at that time. In doing so, he left behind some bitter enemies.

Similarly, there festered a large group of ex-ministers on the back benches with little reason to love Brown. It did not stop them nominating him for leader – perhaps they hoped for a recall, or an eventual peerage, or some other goody – but in their private conversations, one could not doubt their bitterness towards the former Iron Chancellor. Notwithstanding all of these, I must confess that, despite his steamroller approach to politics, Brown has been an extremely successful machine politician.

The question which I and others most frequently asked was: how long can Brown continue to take the incessant punishment dished out to him? Is he like Muhammad Ali, playing his rope-a-dope tactics and aiming to outlast all of his opposition? Alternatively, will he simply retire hurt and punch drunk? For his approach to politics is both highly personal and singular. He has little time for a team, other than as backup to him. I recall one of his former ministers in the Treasury, Helen Liddell, remarking that she could never confirm her diary commitments until the last moment. That was because

Treasury ministers' diary commitments had to be kept flexible to accommodate the last-minute whims of the Chancellor.

Brown's original team was reassigned to some key positions. Whilst Sue Nye – wife of Goldman Sachs honcho Gavin Davies – remained his loyal and effective gatekeeper, his old press secretary, Charlie Whelan, went to work for Unite, Britain's biggest union, where it was believed that he served Brown's interests rather than those of the union's members. Formerly Brown's long-term researchers, Ed Balls and Ed Miliband both became his staunch allies in the Cabinet. Other, newer, supporters were sprinkled liberally throughout the government, with a trusted loyalist strategically placed within every ministerial team.

Whether that was helpful beyond the immediate management and discipline of his government remains a matter for conjecture. Brown had, after all, a mountain to climb if the opinion polls were to be believed. As the incumbent Prime Minister, he was held responsible for both the worst effects of the recession and the public relations disaster of the allowances scandal. In the background, the after-shocks of the Iraq War still reflected on him and on the Labour government. Although there remain doubts about Cameron's Tories to this day, the electoral odds are still stacked in their favour.

This was recognised by a large number of Labour members. Although there are retirees on both sides of the House, it is on the Labour benches where retirement is the most significant phenomenon. Whilst there were those on all sides who were prompted to retire after the expenses scandal, far more Labour members looked at the odds of retaining their seats and decided it was not worth the effort. Others, in safer seats, simply felt that they had had enough. Dissatisfied politically and/or personally, they decided to call it a day. This was hardly a resounding vote of confidence in Labour's chances of re-election.

Nevertheless, the circus always goes on. The real questions were whether or not the pain of the attempt to transmute the Labour Party into a revived Social Democratic Party was worth it, and, secondly, what form the Labour Party is likely to take after the next general election, regardless of the result. Both of these questions are difficult to calibrate. For example, it would be too simplistic to take the massive decline in Labour Party membership as the yardstick of the success or otherwise of New Labour. After all, declining numbers in a political party is neither peculiar to Labour nor to the United Kingdom. Nor has New Labour really been tested electorally yet. Arguably, the elections of 1997 and 2001 were aberrations from what had preceded them. The 2005 election was more in line with the norm of British elections since the war; and that result, whilst giving a clear victory for Labour, had more to do with our sometimes freakish electoral arithmetic and weird representative distribution than an overwhelming mandate. Perhaps Cameron's team is the first serious political challenge that New Labour has faced.

For people like me, New Labour's principal failing was its vacuous emphasis on personality rather than politics, its trite attempts to be all things to all men and women – who will forget Blair's memo demanding that he be associated with any 'good news' stories in government? I cannot forget that at the first Parliamentary Labour Party meeting after the 2001 election, the major lesson for the party, at least according to Barbara Follett, was to do with burnt-out cars. Peter Pike, on the other hand, wanted us to have a policy on housing. At the height of New Labour, it was Barbara rather than Peter who was setting the agenda with my New Labour colleagues, such was the level of thinking and prioritising at which New Labour was operating.

It is only recently that Labour has formally acknowledged again any reference to its traditional commitment to the redistribution of wealth. Predictably, Mandelson was quickly out of the traps to dampen such a misdirection of 'his' project, reaffirming that he was still intensely relaxed about the few getting filthy rich. Yet the notion of redistributing wealth is part of the glue which has held the Labour coalition together for over a hundred years. After all, it is one thing for New Labour to turn its back on one of the party's founders – organised labour – under the wholly misleading catch-all of soundbite of 'modernisation'. It is quite another thing to alienate millions of loyal supporters who looked to redistribution as a vehicle for social justice. Redistribution has always been seen as a key to the aspiration of the bulk of our people for social justice. Without this shared aspiration, the party loses its soul. It becomes merely an alternative, technocratically able management team for running the existing – and often unjust – social order.

To have adopted the belief in the primacy of the market is, to many of us, akin to accepting the law of the jungle. Free market advocates will not be diverted by the moral and literal bankruptcy of the City's financial giants into a recognition that the mantra of 'less regulation', for example, has clearly failed. Better regulation, yes – and more, where it is required. Just dumping regulation for its own sake is a retrograde step by people devoid of the will to bring such financial behemoths into a fairer system, one which is characterised by the overarching importance attached to the common good rather than the indulgence of the greed of the few.

ten

As I amble into the sunset of my parliamentary career, I increasingly embrace the vices of a politician whose best days are well and truly gone. That is, reflection and introspection. I do not, however, share in Enoch Powell's rather opinionated conclusion that all political careers end in tears. His undoubtedly did because of his unfulfilled ambitions. For others, retirement is a sweet release from the drudgery which is a large part of a politician's lot.

Nevertheless, a politician who has spent many years in the public eye would need to be the greatest dullard not to have arrived at some views of public life and those who dabble in it. The validity of those views will, of course, depend on the politician who expresses them and the criticism which certainly follows anyone who dares to rise above the hypocrisy which we call politics. By 'rise above', I mean telling the truth without fearing if that honesty will be a disadvantage in the games which are played between and within parties. By 'hypocrisy', I mean exactly that, as the *Oxford Dictionary* defines it: 'Simulation of virtue; dissimulation; pretence'. In my experience, no other word characterises the political praxis of Parliament better than hypocrisy. The whole of the parliamentary process seems to me to be a battle between those who present truth in one way and their opposition who will twist in another direction whilst both sides affect an objectivity which rarely exists. That is as true of the skirmishes within parties as it is of those between them.

Naturally, my particular concern is the Labour Party and what has happened to it over the forty-six years during which I have been a member. I am more acutely aware of its radical transformation of it during the twenty-five years of my full-time political career. I use the word 'career' hesitantly – at one time, I believed that it was a vocation rather than a career to be a full-time politician. I have learnt that, even for those who began their political lives with the flame of idealism lighting their way, that flame was very often quickly snuffed out as career opportunity raised its ugly head. That is the political world we have in our country. It will get worse after the next election.

When I became involved in the Labour Party in the swinging sixties, it still saw itself as a mass party. In many wards and constituencies, there were large numbers of often only nominal members. Some of those joined via Labour social clubs, the rules of which demanded membership of the Labour Party to qualify for membership of the club. Yet the party was generally active at a local level, with people keen to attend and hold office. Parallel to this was the trade union movement, a rich recruiting ground for new Labour Party members and relevant in its own right to individuals and communities. Even the co-operative movement maintained its relevance to working-class families throughout the land.

By the 1980s, Thatcherism was the order of the day in public life. The economic landscape had shifted, and with it the industrial profile of the nation. Unions were under the cosh and in rapid retreat from the power and numbers they had commanded during the 1970s. The stresses spread from wider society into the Labour Party, complicating Labour's internal battles, firstly between right and left and then with Militant. Along came New Labour, in a last ditch attempt to win power before the Labour Party splintered after a feared defeat in 1997.

It worked – at least for a while. What it also did, however, was to emasculate Labour ideologically. New Labour became a brand, devoid of substance, but sold successfully to a bedazzled electorate who were tired of the Tory brand and their painful remedies to our national ills. No one can deny the marketing exercise success that was New Labour. Unfortunately, snake oil salesmen are always found out eventually; and New Labour's day of reckoning is nigh.

What, therefore, will be at the core of the Labour Party after the next election? Not a great deal, I fear. One only has to look at the way in which the party has recruited its front line troops to fight in 2010. Political correctness is still pushed in preference to political reality, giving us more women candidates but a weaker fighting force. Formerly safe Labour seats have been earmarked by a monomaniac Harriet Harman – in charge of the selection process – for all-women shortlists. In many of these seats, it has resulted in as few as three or four applicants coming forward – hardly a large enough pool of talent from which a good candidate might be chosen.

Compounding the difficulty, it appears that in many vacated seats, the majority of the applicants originate from London. With the greatest respect to Londoners, the politics – indeed, the thinking – in London is very different from that of the provinces. We mere provincials need London-based candidates with a London social, cultural and political perspective like we need a hole in the head.

Ah, you might say, if they are individually good candidates, what does it matter? After all, Parliament deals with national issues and it meets in London. That is precisely the problem facing the future Parliamentary Labour Party. It will consist largely, if not of Londoners, then of people based in London. That tendency will be reinforced by the emerging proposed changes to the parliamentary allowances which will render the possibility of provincial members living in their constituencies ever more difficult. The only people who will be able to afford to sit in the Commons will be those who are resident in London.

Thus, it seems likely that the Parliamentary Labour Party after the election may have more women members, but that its overall quality will be even lower than it is today. Its members will also be more likely to be people who live in London, lending the PLP an even more London-centric view of the needs of the nation. It is likely to have even fewer people who are traditional trade unionists or from the lower social orders. It will, therefore, be a narrower cross-section of the people it purports to represent, and far removed from its traditional roots. It will make the present collection of old Etonians on the Conservative front bench look remarkably representative of the British people.

Collectively, they will spearhead a party which in many parts of the country is on its knees. In common with other political parties, Labour struggles for membership and, as a result, is a far cry from the proud boast of being a mass party. Its finances are in a parlous state, making it more dependent on trade union support than ever. Yet those trade unions have themselves contracted in number, members and resources. Moreover, the burning wish of the 'New' Labour faction to sever Labour Party links with the trade unions has led a number of unions to disaffiliate from the Labour Party, including the RMT and the FBU. There are growing voices in others – such as Unison – demanding that their union follows suit and stop paying monies into Labour.

A Conservative government would, without doubt, make the financing of the Labour Party even more difficult. At the same time it would slash the overall number of parliamentary seats, to the further discomfiture of Labour. At the very least, these developments would cause major shifts within the Labour Party and major disagreements. Perhaps the powerful Scottish bloc of Labour members would be broken up. Equally likely, a redistribution of fewer parliamentary seats would hit the traditional geographic heartlands of Labour dramatically. More than ever, the Labour Party inside Parliament would view its role through the prism of London and the south-east – the part of the country where the wealth, the people and the seats are.

Yet when those metropolitan members turn to the union movement for financial support – having done little or nothing for them whilst in office – they will face trade union leading lights from the provinces. The union leaders themselves are caught between a Labour Party leadership which, to all intents and purposes, dismisses them contemptuously, and a need and desire to influence that leadership in its policy development. This is not a dynamic tension, but a destructive one. It will take immense political skill to navigate a way through these contradictory tendencies. On the one side will be 'New' Labour – metropolitan, middle class, sold on image and personality. Facing them will remain 'Old'

Labour – mainly provincial, ideological, given to utopian hopes of the state. Presumably leading the two factions will be the rising stars of the current government.

Whatever happens after the 2010 election, the old guard will go. There will be no Brown, Darling or Straw at the top for long. I suspect Harman will linger on. Indeed, many believe she sees herself as a future leader. Hence the accusation that she has been packing all-women shortlists with an eye to their support in a future leadership contest. Johnson will be consigned to the 'too old' scrapheap. It will be for the 'Young Turks' of Gordon Brown's government to take up the baton of leadership.

The question that must be asked is whether or not they are capable of the demands facing the Labour Party? After all, it is a common view that Brown has packed his Cabinet and government with people who, in some cases, have no experience and no politics – people unlikely to trouble him, but rather to acquiesce readily to his wishes. It is from amongst such that the party will be expected to choose.

These are not the great characters, the politicians 'with a hinterland', of yesteryear. In fact, I believe the present Cabinet to be the least politically able Labour Cabinet or shadow Cabinet in my lifetime. Why is this, you might ask? Surely the edges would have been knocked off them by virtue of holding high office alone? Not so, say I. They have no comparators in the real world, since so many of them have little or no experience outside the world of politics. I have nothing against researchers, special advisers, marketing or advertising people; but these occupations do not entail real life experience with which the electorate can identify. It shows in the decisions taken, the postures adopted and the ignorance of human nature so often exhibited by bright, keen, but woefully out of touch young ministers.

The current Cabinet is replete with former researchers – the

Miliband brothers, Burnham and Balls figure in the list. A further section of it consists of people who have risen without trace – people like Alexander, Murphy and Byrne. There is the lightweight (or makeweight) tendency including Jowell, Bradshaw and Ainsworth. There are not many left to consider as serious politicians; but it is from the ranks of these that a new leadership is expected to emerge, facing Labour's greatest challenges in eighty years.

In government, the Labour Party has already handicapped itself in a variety of ways, by sins of both omission and commission. It has narrowed the gene pool of its potential members of Parliament and it has alienated its backers. It has altered the Commons' procedures in such as way as to make opposition – if it comes – an impossible task. We have given away any realistic hope of a dominant Labour representation of the United Kingdom in Europe. In a post-electoral world, we might even face being squeezed out of the devolved legislatures, as well as from the national parliament.

In the country at large, the 'New' Labour project has done even more damage. Voters are more discerning than so-called strategists give them credit for. Thus, back in 1994, when Mandelson and Gould were arguing that Labour's traditional voters had nowhere else to go, they were wrong. In fact, the arrogance of their approach encouraged two alternatives: voting for fringe parties like the BNP, or simply opting out of voting altogether and staying at home.

This has not only led to a worrying presence of the BNP in places like Burnley and Stoke, it has given the BNP seats in the European Parliament, to our national shame. Labour councillors have taken a beating throughout the land, with traditionally Labour towns and cities going over to the Tories or the Liberal Democrats. This shift in local priorities has been in inverse proportion to New Labour's zeal for national party reform.

Can this contradiction between New Labour zealotry and the more traditional Labour principles and values be reconciled? I fear not – it is a battle between very different political philosophies (if that is not too grand a word). The choice for the Labour Party is between the social democratic urges of New Labour – complete with deregulation, devotion to markets and privatisation – and the democratic socialist model which calls for regulation, appropriate intervention and a thriving public sector. There can be no compromise between the two.

Unfortunately, the Labour Party does not have the luxury of time to contemplate its ideological navel. The fear of 1994 has returned: a shattering defeat in the forthcoming general election might lead to the splintering of the Labour Party and the wider Labour movement. The first priority is to do everything possible to contain the massive Tory threat in the 2010 election.

It was for this reason that there was little enthusiasm for the Hoon/Hewitt attempted putsch against Brown. It was certainly not out of love or even respect for the party leader. Labour members realised that a leadership contest might have settled some people's personal grudges, but it would have done nothing to help Labour at the general election. Even if the polls are right – and there is little point in questioning their consistency – and the Tories are hot favourites to win, there remains a strong possibility of a small majority, or even no majority at all. Given the history of recent years, I would see that as quite an achievement for Labour.

For lurking behind the ballot box is the reality of the recession. All serious commentators – and most politicians – see dire times ahead. Whoever holds the reins of government will have extremely tough decisions to make, involving cuts, tax increases and job losses. The severity of the demands to be made on government, and the possibility of a government with a narrow majority, or a hung Parliament, make for some intriguing possible scenarios.

Some have even suggested a national government to carry the country through these turbulent times. That is highly unlikely, although whoever is in charge of the national shop will be taking an enormous gamble politically. The query many have is about who will carry the electoral can for the forthcoming austerity? Some Labour people actually believe it is in the party's longer term interest to be in opposition when the controversy hits the fan. Their thinking is that the government of the day will crash under the pressure, leaving the opposition to collect the electoral benefit. The underlying assumption is that the electorate is dim-witted, with the memory of a clapped-out computer. I do not share this view.

I would be keen to see, in the event of a general election defeat, a root-and-branch clearout of those in leading positions (this would be my personal preference even if we won). We do, however, have a set of rules which insist on the political beauty contest of the parliamentary committee elections. If I am right, the people electing that committee will have far more in common with the current tranche of leading lights than the old Labour diehards would ever have had. This is the measure of the change in the Labour Party. Blair, Mandelson et al. set out to rebuild Labour in their own image and likeness. By and large, they have succeeded.

Outsiders like Jon Cruddas are sometimes tipped as a fresh hope for the party. I myself nominated Jon for the post of deputy leader (mostly, I admit, on the grounds that he was not one of the 'usual suspects'). He quickly moved to dampen expectations of himself. Now this could be a laudable streak of humility in a leadership hopeful. On the other hand, it could be a tactic, or even an evasion of responsibility. I do not know, and only time will tell. What is remarkable is that Jon – himself a former special adviser in Downing Street – is the only name to have surfaced as a future hopeful from outside the magic governmental circle in recent years.

This points to the dearth of talent raised through Labour ranks over the past sixteen years. Those who did flourish are either past their sell-by date, not up to speed, or – as in most cases – both. More fundamentally, what happens to a political party devoid of leadership talent? The noble Lord Mandelson will undoubtedly try to foist on the party – and, hence, the country – a 'product', as he has tried (and so far failed) to do with David Miliband. Sadly for him, both the 'New' Labour brand, and spin itself, are forever tarnished in the eyes of the electorate. It will take more than a ready smile and an advertising slogan to convince people a second time around.

So, the pain goes on, and will do for the foreseeable future for those who experienced the vintage days of Labour. The painful price has meant a national shift rightwards, with less compassion for those at the bottom of the heap, a reduced regard for what government can achieve and a much diminished electoral base for progressive and redistributive policies. Have the years of Labour government been worth the political suffering for Labour Party members like me? I hazard a guess that they have not, despite the successes. If we were to weigh in the scales the fulfilment of the personal ambitions of Brown and Blair against the longer term interests of the majority of the nation and of the Labour Party, I know on which side the balance would fall.

postscript

Since writing *Labour Pains*, I have decided to stand down as a candidate in the 2010 general election. Already I feel a weight lifted, as several colleagues who are also standing down have described their relief. Even so, there was a touch of farce in how I resigned.

I had intended to make a formal announcement at my constituency party's monthly general committee meeting. However, the meeting was cancelled – or rather, never called. This is typical of so much of the present-day Labour Party and adds to my concerns about what faces us all after the next election.

Make no mistake: regardless of the outcome of the 2010 general election, the next government will be subject to two unavoidable realities. Firstly, given the global economic crisis, that government will be forced to make the kind of economic adjustments that will cause great pain, particularly for those people whence I sprang and on whose I behalf I have tried to be a voice.

Secondly, whichever party ends up governing, the next government will be highly centralised and packed with people with limited experience (if any) of the lives of the mass of those they will claim to represent. To put it bluntly, the economic crisis will be matched by a crisis of confidence in the ability of the next government to understand what the electorate needs and wants.

I will not now be a part of the concomitant great debates. My decision to step down puts me in the same position as the vast majority of my fellow British citizens: a bystander, whilst the great and the good decide what they believe is in the best interests of the rest of us.

The reader might ask: is it a dereliction of duty for me to retreat from the debates which are bound to ensue over the coming months and years? Not at all. Having concluded that it is time for others to make their decisions for the future of the country, as my generation eases into its sunset years, it is nothing but a recognition that all things must pass. A new generation of politicians ought to reflect the exigencies of their life, times and values.

It strikes me that the changes which have taken place in politics are symptomatic of those which have occurred in wider society. Today's consumerism and materialism have infected other areas. Worse still, the Warhol aphorism that we might all have our fifteen minutes of fame has done more than anything to distort our expectation of more substantive and positive outcomes in life.

Anyone who watches current television and sees politicians prostituting themselves on reality shows (I have been guilty of this myself) will appreciate how debased the presentation of serious issues has become. What is more, the cult of celebrity has overtaken the need for the serious and substantive discussion of issues. I cannot live politically with such a superficial approach to the great challenges with which we are faced.

Perhaps this is partly to do with a generational shift. When colleagues text, Twitter and use Facebook as a matter of course, priding themselves on their instantaneous communication of the trite and the superfluous, it replaces a more considered and reflective approach to the business of our times with an air of redundancy and the charge of irrelevance.

My particular concern upon leaving Parliament is that it is a much-maligned institution, albeit maligned with good cause. Yet it is the principal check which we have on a marauding executive. That executive will continue to prey on the citizenry of this country, regardless of which party is in power. That is the nature of government in Britain, from Charles I to Gordon Brown. A neutered House of Commons – which it surely is – is a metaphor for a neutered democracy.

On a purely personal level, I want to add no legitimacy as a member of Parliament to a virtually defunct and ineffective institution. I take the view, long expressed by others, that participation in its charades only encourages those who abuse our political institutions. As I walk away, perhaps as an ageing and increasingly cynical retiree, I ask myself just one question. Was it worth it?